KU-652-913

TORCH BIBLE
COMMENTARIES
(*Apocrypha*)

General Editors

THE REV. JOHN MARSH, D.PHIL.
Principal of Mansfield College, Oxford

THE REV. CANON ALAN RICHARDSON, D.D.
*Professor of Christian Theology in the University of
Nottingham*

FOREWORD TO SERIES

The aim of this series of commentaries on books of the Bible is to provide the general reader with the soundest possible assistance in understanding the message of each book considered as a whole and as a part of the Bible.

The findings and views of modern critical scholarship on the text of the Bible have been taken fully into account; but we have asked the writers to remember that the Bible is more than a quarry for the practice of erudition; that it contains the message of the living God.

We hope that intelligent people of varying interests will find that these commentaries, while not ignoring the surface difficulties, are able to concentrate the mind on the essential Gospel contained in the various books of the Bible.

Volumes in the series include

THE WISDOM OF SOLOMON

Introduction and Commentary

by

JOHN GEYER

SCM PRESS LTD
BLOOMSBURY STREET LONDON

To

IAN

Leader of the Rebels,
Son of my sorrow,
Son of my joy

UNIVERSITY
LIBRARY
NOTTINGHAM

FIRST PUBLISHED 1963

© SCM PRESS LTD 1963

PRINTED IN GREAT BRITAIN BY
NORTHUMBERLAND PRESS LIMITED
GATESHEAD ON TYNE

6001318502
206614

CONTENTS

COMMENTARY

Part One: WISDOM IN PRACTICE

*Chapter and
Verse*

Chapter and
Verse

Part Two: HYMN TO WISDOM

Part Three: A PHILOSOPHY OF HISTORY

Chapter and
Verse

PREFACE

As this is the first book that the author has had published, he wishes to record his gratitude to all those who have helped him on the way to make this possible. He refrains from mentioning names, as there are few amongst the great who would be flattered by the dedication of this little book, and indeed they might blush to be associated with so slight a work. But his thanks are due to those to whom he owes much: to his parents, without whom nothing would have been possible; to the staff of Silcoates School, who gave him his first grounding in biblical theology; to his friends there, who made him happy; to the Fellows and his fellow-students at Queen's College, Cambridge; to his tutors at Oriel and Mansfield Colleges, Oxford, and especially to the Attic Community; to his Professor and many friends in the University of Heidelberg, especially those of the Ecumenical Institute, who are now scattered to many parts of the world; above all to his congregation in St Andrews, who perfected his joy in life by calling him to be a minister, and who also readily made it possible for him to write this book; and to his colleague who came to help him out with the pastoral work whilst this book was written.

Many are the authors whose researches have been drawn on in the writing of this commentary, and those mainly consulted have been listed in the short bibliography. As this series of studies is intended for the inexpert reader, the author has avoided detailed footnotes, in his attempt to make this account of the Wisdom of Solomon as clear as possible.

BIBLIOGRAPHY

B. M. Metzger, *Introduction to the Apocrypha*, New York 1957, provides an elementary background to the various books of the Apocrypha.

E. Bevan, *Jerusalem under the High-Priests*, London 1904, is a delightfully written book, covering the period with great insight and knowledge.

O. S. Rankin, *Israel's Wisdom Literature*, Edinburgh, reprint 1954, is a classical work covering the different strands of thought running through this period.

Among the commentaries J. A. F. Gregg, Cambridge Bible for Schools 1909, is very learned and useful. C. Harris, in Chas. Gore's *New Commentary on Holy Scripture*, SPCK 1929, is brief. S. Holmes in R. H. Charles' *The Apocrypha and Pseudepigrapha Vol. I*, Oxford 1913 (unwieldy and unobtainable) has written an amusing Introduction, and comments mainly on textual matters. I have also consulted J. Fichtner in O. Eissfeldt's *Handbuch* series 1938, which is beset with the notion of literary types, and P. Heinisch *Das Buch der Weisheit*, Münster 1912, which stands a fair chance of being the best piece of expository work on any book in any language to date. J. Reider *Book of Wisdom*, New York 1957, is very good for beginners.

INTRODUCTION

Today there are comparatively few people who read their bibles, and there are even fewer who have an Apocrypha to read. But those who do turn to the Wisdom of Solomon will find that it is one of the greatest books ever written.

There are many ways of judging greatness in literature. *Wisdom* belongs to that class of books which, when a man reads them, he must pause every now and then to praise his Maker; books which give him a grasp of the values of life, and open to him the untold riches of the world; books which make him want to reach out and possess eternity.

There are not many people now who feel they want to do any of these things. The search for spiritual truth sometimes seems to be the pursuit of a quieter age that has passed. This century is alight with the possibilities of the present world order. The physical world presses in, real and earnest. The political world is a challenge to all serious-minded people. Changes have come so rapidly during the past decades that men must speak of a new world, and religion and piety have to a large measure passed away with the old world.

But this is not the first age of transition that the world has passed through, and the Wisdom of Solomon was written in a period which had problems similar to those of the twentieth century. There were great movements afoot which made people dissatisfied with the old forms of religion and the traditional ideas. People had discovered in the world around them beauty, mystery and excitement that had been neglected through the ages. New questions arose which could not be answered by the wisdom inherited from the past.

With the coming of a new era people reacted in different ways. Some refused to budge from the position that they and their families had held for generations. Some went to the other extreme and said there was no good whatever in the old faith,

13

and replaced it in their thinking with a secular philosophy. But there was a way between the two extremes. The middle way was by far the most difficult because it meant that some serious thinking had to be done. It involved working out afresh what the old faith was saying, and discovering how far it was still true. To do this demanded an open and tolerant mind. This was the way that the author of *Wisdom* chose to go.

For the meaning and purpose of a book to be plain to the reader it must be put in its context. Something must be learnt of where it comes from, the times in which it was written, and what sort of man wrote it. In the present case something must be added to the list about the collection of books to which this one belongs. As this is the first of the Torch Commentaries to be written on an Apocryphal book some readers may be wondering what the Apocrypha is.

THE APOCRYPHA

The Apocrypha is a collection of books which in some
bibles is printed between the Old Testament and the New
Testament and in other bibles is not printed at all. The reason
for this is that the Church has never been able to make up
its mind whether these books should be regarded as holy or
not.

and in some is printed a part of the O.T.

This raises the question of why any books should be
regarded as holy scripture. Many books were written, but few
were chosen as holy. The Old Testament, as it stands in
English bibles, was taken over by the Church from the Jewish
religion. These books had come to have a special place in the
national life and religion and at a special council held at
Jamnia in AD 90 the Jewish fathers proclaimed these books as
canonical. That is to say, they recognized them as containing
the Word that God had spoken to his people in the course
of many generations. Later the Christian Church added to
these its own collection of holy scriptures which came to be
known as the New Testament.

Very closely associated with the books of the Old Testament, which were recognized by the council at Jamnia, were
some others. Like the rest of the Old Testament in those days
they were mainly read in Greek, as the original Hebrew in
which they were written had been a dead language for some
centuries. In these Greek versions of the Old Testament some
of the books that are now collected together as the Apocrypha
were included, scattered amongst the other books.

These Apocryphal books were certainly used by early Christians, and some of them are quoted in the New Testament.
But they had a varied history. Christians in the east, that is
to say, the Greek Church, quoted from them less and less as
time went on. In the west they continued to be highly regarded,
but they were not thought to be as inspired as the Old Testa-

ment itself. The great reformer Martin Luther estimated the value of the Apocrypha rather low, because there were passages which seemed to contradict the great truths of the other scriptures which he had re-discovered for the Church. This stirred up the Roman Catholic Church, which promptly proclaimed most of the Apocrypha to be canonical. This was stated at the Council of Trent in 1546. The Church of England, true to her tradition, took the middle way and said that the Apocrypha would be all right so long as it was used for instruction and not as an authority for establishing doctrine. In 1647 the Presbyterian Church, assembled at Westminster, said that the books of the Apocrypha were no better than any other books, and certainly not as good as the books in the bible.

So the reader is left to make up his own mind: whether he will adopt the opinion of the tradition in which he stands, or whether he will take up these books to see for himself whether there is anything of worth in them.

The word Apocrypha is a Greek word which means ' things hidden away '. Theories why these things were hidden away have varied. At first it was said that they were hidden because they were so profound that they must only be shown to the initiated. Later it was said that they were hidden because they were not fit to be read.

The Apocrypha is available to English readers in various translations, including the *Authorized Version* (on which the present commentary is based), the *Revised Version* and the *Revised Standard Version*. The New English Bible translation is being prepared.

GENERAL INTRODUCTION

DATE

According to most scholars *Wisdom* was written some time during the first century before Christ. The reasons for thinking that it was not written before this are that there are quotations in it that have been made from the Greek translation of the Old Testament, agreeing with this, though differing from the Hebrew. Also, there is a suggestion in *Wisdom* that the Jews had been persecuted a few years previously, and this is generally understood to refer to the persecution under Physcon Ptolemy at the end of the second century. Since Paul and other New Testament writers were familiar with the book it must have been written by their time. As the Roman emperors controlled the world and were friendly towards the Jews after 30 BC it is not likely to have been written after that date.

AUTHOR

If *Wisdom* was written in the first century before Christ it clearly cannot have been written by Solomon, who died about nine hundred years before that time. Who wrote it? When Origen asked the same question about the author of the Epistle to the Hebrews he was forced to the conclusion that God alone knows, and the scholars have reached a fair amount of agreement amongst themselves that this is the best answer to the question of the authorship of *Wisdom*.

Why, then, is the book called 'The Wisdom of Solomon' if

Solomon did not write it? The book is certainly written as though it had come from the hand of the Hebrew king (cf. 7.5; 8.14; 9.7), though the actual name of Solomon is never mentioned other than in the title. There are two main reasons which can be given for the association of the book with Solomon. The first is that it was the custom of the times to write under an assumed name. This seems to have been mainly because the Jews had not added to their sacred books for some centuries and people who wished to write imitated the old masters rather than used their own names. The custom may have started in earlier times when the author would have been in danger of persecution by the Gentile authorities if his name had been known. This was a definite possibility at the time when the Book of Daniel was written. The second reason why our book is ascribed to Solomon is that all Wisdom was traced back to him. The reader will be familiar with books in the Old Testament which were written about this time which are also said to be of Solomon (Prov.; Eccles.). This tradition is based on the story in I Kings 3 about how Solomon chose Wisdom as the best gift that God could give him. Even this story probably developed long after Solomon had been dead and buried, but the fact remains that in the period when our book was written Solomon was regarded as the father of all Israel's Wisdom, as he still is by pious Jews. Speaking of the use of Solomon's name one scholar remarks: 'This is, of course, a literary device, and would deceive no one. But it made the book anonymous, and anonymous it remains' (Holmes, p. 525).

But although we cannot give the author a name, we can discover a good deal about the sort of man he was from what he has written. He was a Jew living in the great city of Alexandria in Egypt. There was a great Jewish Colony in those parts, and many of the Jews there were moving with the times and adopting the ways of the Greek world and culture which surrounded them. Alexandria was a city which had been built by Alexander the Great when he was extending the culture of his own country over the huge empire that he ruled, an empire which included Egypt. Our author was not so enthusiastic about these new-fangled ways as some of his friends were, and he wrote his book to appeal to his fellow Jews to remain faithful to the true religion. He got a good deal of amusement from observing the Greeks, and no doubt he hoped that what he had to say would appeal to some of the best Gentile thinkers as well. But his main purpose was to consolidate, not to expand, the community to which he belonged.

GREEKS AND HEBREWS

Something must also be said about the affairs of the Jews in Palestine for two centuries before Wisdom was written. Since 411 BC the Jews had been busy putting their country in order after they had been allowed to return from exile in Babylon by the Persians, who were the new conquerors of the eastern world. But they were not left in peace for long. At the beginning of the fourth century before Christ Alexander arrived as the spear-head of western expansion. The Greeks were good colonizers. They were very cultured people and had a great deal to offer. When they went out east they were concerned at the standard of living that they found there and tried to improve it. They built splendid cities and put up public baths and eating places which were very popular. Both the men and women eagerly found out the latest fashions in clothes and hair style, and the Greek way of life seemed to be well on the way to replacing the Hebrew tradition. But not all the Jews welcomed these changes. They remembered the faith of their fathers, and were determined that Alexander should not stand between them and the living God. They took exception to many things. One of the greatest complaints that the writer of I Macc. had was that the Greeks built a gymnasium in Jerusalem. The Greeks had a deep appreciation of the human body whilst the Jews were by tradition rather self-conscious about it. Another matter which caused a great deal

latter
part of
C4d.

of unrest was the fact that the followers of the new mode wore hats. Why this should upset the Jews is difficult to understand. But it did.

Anyway, through one cause or another, tension grew, and rival parties emerged on the scene. Finally the storm burst with the arrival of Antiochus Epiphanes, Greek overlord of Syria and Palestine. His name means Antiochus the Manifested or, in full, the Manifested God. But the Jews who did not like him called him Antiochus Epimanes, which means Antiochus the Mad. Much had happened by this time, nearly two hundred years since Alexander had come to Palestine. When Alexander died his empire was divided between three rulers. Those with whom this study is mainly concerned were the Seleucids, who took over Syria and the eastern part of the empire, and the Ptolemies, who took over Egypt. Palestine lay between the two, which was and is the root cause of the tragedy of its long history. The Ptolemies and the Seleucids were always fighting over Palestine, and that is why people like Antiochus spent so much time trying to get a firm grasp on the country. Otherwise there would not have been much to bother about in this little but obdurate land. Antiochus seemed to think that it would strengthen his cause if the people had an image of him in the temple. A modern reader is reminded of the photographs of leaders used in parades in totalitarian countries. But Antiochus intended more than this. The people were to worship him as the divine emperor, and in this way he hoped to consolidate the national life around his own figure. But some Jews, instead of worshipping this object, called it the Abomination of Desolation. Their refusal to co-operate resulted in a persecution. The Jews fought back, a number of them rallying round Judas Maccabaeus, who led the guerilla warfare that followed. Eventually Judas gained control of the temple and it was rededicated. After this the Jews enjoyed a certain amount of freedom from oppression until the rise of the next rulers of the world, the Romans, when they had to start all over again.

Two distinct kinds of Judaism emerged from this period. On

the one hand there were the rich people who delighted in new fashions. They knew that if they kept in with the rulers their own position would be secure. They accepted the Greek customs and costumes, but at the same time continued their worship in the temple. Living in Jerusalem they enjoyed a good deal of influence, and a very comfortable living. They were the Jewish counterpart of the Greek sceptics and emerge in the New Testament as the Sadducees headed by the high-priest. On the other hand, there were those who treasured the old ways and became more Jewish than they had ever been before. They took the line which Orwell said was the basic element of British comics: that all foreigners are funny. Their religion centred not on the temple in Jerusalem, but on the local synagogue. Their chief delight was the Law, that is to say the first five books of the bible, and they added to this many more laws to explain the ones that they already had. These people emerge in the New Testament as the Pharisees, and they were good people, though anyone reading Matt. 23 will have to admit that they had their shortcomings.

ALEXANDRIA

The Greeks had the biggest empire to date. The fact that everybody spoke the same language made travel very easy, and there was a lot of coming and going. Many Jews left Palestine and went to live in other places and this began the great dispersion of Jewry which is a familiar, and welcome aspect of the contemporary world. One of the biggest centres of the Jewish dispersion was Alexandria. In this city three worlds met: the Egyptian, the Jewish and the Greek. They were located in different parts of the town, but even so each had an influence over the other. The biggest library in the ancient world had been built there. The Jews used it and became familiar with the Greek authors who wrote most of the books in stock. In this way Alexandria became a bridge between the two cultures which had developed in Palestine,

and which were affecting Jews wherever they were settled
throughout the Greek world. Alexandria was not a place of
high passions, except during the university rags. People had
time to think things out in a quiet atmosphere, and the Jews
who were living there were able to come to terms with the
new world. One of the first things they did in Alexandria was
to translate the bible, or at any rate the first five books of it,
from Hebrew into Greek. This translation was used by Jews
throughout the world and it was the one that St Paul used.
It gained a mystic authority as venerable as that which the
Authorized Version holds in the minds of some people today.
The Jews revered it until the time when the Christians started
using it as the divine text from which they laboured to prove
that Jesus was the Messiah they had been waiting for. The
rabbis took the usual line of defence and said that the Greek
version was after all a poor translation, and that in the
original something else was meant. So the Hebrew scriptures
have been read in the synagogue ever since.

. But this is to look beyond our period. Wisdom belongs to
the time when Greek was in the ascendancy. Now, the Greeks
were a highly intellectual people. They placed philosophy on
a higher rung than manual labour, and also held it to be
superior to popular religion. The ordinary people of Greece
still accepted the myths about gods and goddesses which were
traditional to their country. The myths had very little moral
content. The deities were represented as eating and drinking
and being generally immoral. The philosophers had a much
more exalted view of things and believed in one god only.
This god they referred to as 'The Being' and considered that
he had nothing to do with time or space or the world or anything material, except that it started them all off in the first
place. The philosophers considered themselves akin to this
god through their minds and souls. This spiritual element in
man they held to be imprisoned in their bodies from which
it must be liberated, so that it could escape above the material
world to the place where The Being lived. The only way to
make this escape was through philosophy. A high standard of

moral behaviour was involved in their teaching, because they
believed that the people who were most like The Being were
the good people.

When the Greeks met the Jews they began to find out something about the Hebrew religion and like many modern
readers of the Old Testament they had great difficulty in
accepting many parts of it. They had no liking for a God
who had hands and arms and who spoke like a human being.
There was too much of this world in the religion of the Jews.
But the Jews have always been equal to any attack, whether
physical or intellectual, and a counter-attack was worked out,
mainly in Alexandria. Their reply was that the stories of the
Old Testament were not to be taken at their face value. They
had been written in a special way so that the Greeks would
not be able to understand them. Really all these gruesome
stories were symbols of great spiritual truths. That is, they
were allegories which had to be interpreted in order to get
at the meaning. This method did not gather full strength until
Philo came on the scene, after *Wisdom* had been written, and
not much use is made of allegory in this book. But eventually
the Jews decided that this was the right answer to their difficulties, and having once made a start they warmed to their
task. They went so far as to claim that Plato, who was so
highly esteemed by the Greek philosophers, was indebted for
his material to Moses. Where evidence was scanty they invented it.

In this way the Jews of Alexandria presented their religion
to intelligent Greeks and many converts were made. They
themselves learnt quite a few useful things from the Greeks,
and some of the ideas found in *Wisdom* are due to the influence of Greek philosophers. Alexandria was a door through
which a man might go in and out between the Hebrew and
the Greek world. This tradition remained in Alexandria in
Christian times and the damage done to the Christian religion
because of it remains to this day. The danger was noted by
Tertullian in the third century, but no one took any notice
then, and there are still theologians who think that philosophy

can lead us to God. What Tertullian said was this: ' Worldly
wisdom culminates in philosophy with its rash interpretation
of God's nature and purpose. It is philosophy which supplies
the heresies with their equipment. From philosophy come the
aeons and those infinite forms—whatever they are—and
Valentinus's human trinity. He had been a Platonist. From
philosophy came Marcion's God, the better for his inactivity.
He had come from the Stoics. The idea of an immortal soul
had come from the Epicureans, and the denial of the resurrection of the flesh was taken over from the common tradition
of the philosophical schools. Zeno taught them to equate God
and matter, and Heracleitus comes on the scene when anything is being laid down about a god of fire . . . A plague on
Aristotle, who taught them dialectic, the art which destroys
as much as it builds . . . It reconsiders every point to make
sure it never finishes a discussion . . . What has Jerusalem to
do with Athens? '[1]

ABOUT *WISDOM*

For the most part *Wisdom* is a well written book. It is clear
in thought and expression. The author avoids undue emotion
and obscurantism. The book falls into three main divisions.

Part I (chapters 1-5) shows the practical uses of Wisdom.
People who have it are happier than people who don't. Also,
it is the source of immortality. At the end of time, when the
world is summed up, the wicked people who have avoided
Wisdom in this world will find that they have put their trust
in all the wrong things. The righteous, who have Wisdom, will
be shown to have been right all the time.

Part II (chapters 6-9) is written in praise of Wisdom. Wisdom is here presented as a woman who is a true lover of men
and courts their company. Wisdom and Mankind are two

[1] From the translation of Tertullian's ' Prescriptions Against Heretics ' by
S. L. Greenslade in The Library of Christian Classics, Vol. V *Early Latin
Theology* SCM, 1956, pp. 35-6.

partners. Her character is described, and in the last chapter (9) 'Solomon'—as we shall continue to call the author of this book when moved to name him—prays that he may receive Wisdom.

Part III (chapters 10-19) loses something of the simplicity of the other two parts and the author is inclined to wander. But his purpose is clear enough. He sets out to show how Wisdom has guided the affairs of nations through history, bringing good rewards to the righteous and bad fortune to the wicked. This is set out in a series of contrasts, firstly between the righteous and the evil in Israel, and secondly between Israel and other nations, especially the Egyptians. The references to Egypt would be of special interest to the readers in Alexandria. The escape of Israel from Egypt many centuries before was and is kept alive in Jewish minds through their Passover Festival which takes place each year. This section contains a subsection (chapters 13-15) which deals with the foolishness of worshipping idols.

Some scholars think that Part III was not written by the unknown author of Parts I and II but by another unknown author. There is good reason for this contention. It has already been noted that the style of the last part of the book is more obscure than the earlier chapters. Also Parts I and II are more under the influence of Greek thought than Part III, and they speak more of God's mercy than of his judgment. Part III shows a greater sense of Israel's unique place in the history of the world. Especially noticeable is the fact that in 1₽2 God appears as the chief agent rather than Wisdom. The theological significance of this will be pointed out in the next section. But the reader need not worry unduly which unknown author he is reading. Part III arises quite naturally from Parts I-II and develops on a larger scale what has been worked out there.

Some scholars think the ending of the book (19.22) is rather abrupt, and suggest that the real ending has been lost. This, however, is a matter of opinion, and there is no evidence that 19.22 is not the ending originally intended.

THE IDEAS

As has already been said, *Wisdom* was written at a time when people were asking questions. This is a familiar trend of our own times. No sooner is one question resolved than a whole lot of other questions arise out of the answer. The books produced at the time of *Wisdom* attempted to present theology more systematically than had been tried before. The ideas which concerned 'Solomon' were very similar to the questions that people are asking today.

WHAT IS WISDOM?

Throughout this introduction the word Wisdom has been used with a capital letter, and it has appeared in some strange contexts. The reader may well be wondering whether it means what he always thought it meant. 'Wisdom' usually means understanding the ways of the world and going canny.

To the Hebrew Wisdom was an occupation of a professional class called the Wise, though the benefits of it could be had by the general public, rather as medicine is got from a doctor. The Wise took their place alongside of the priest and the prophet (Jer. 18.18). But whereas the priests and prophets reach back to the earliest times of Israel's history the Wise do not appear until the reign of King Hezekiah (725-697 BC)[1]. They had, however, long been familiar figures at the courts of other oriental kings. They were kept at court so that the king could ask for their advice which was based on a store of learning. They would no doubt act as his secretaries and teach his children as well. Also they were very useful for

[1] The Wise have generally been associated with the reign of Solomon, which is certainly the biblical tradition (1 Kings 3), but this view has recently been challenged by R. B. Y. Scott in his essay 'Solomon and the Beginnings of Wisdom in Israel' in *Wisdom in Israel and the Ancient Near East*, essays presented to H. H. Rowley, Brill, 1955, pp. 262-279.

interpreting difficult dreams. In Israel they worked with the scribes, and they were learned in the Law.

The sort of thing that these people dealt in to begin with was short proverbs many of which are preserved in the Book of Proverbs. Children would probably have to learn them and copy them in school. The proverbs, often illustrations drawn from everyday life, taught one how to become healthy, wealthy and wise, chiefly by being good. Later these were expanded into quite long books dealing with problems, such as the Book of Job.

The basic philosophy of these schools of Wisdom was that small things go wrong in life because people are not fully aware of what is involved. The proverbs were intended to help people through. When it came to the major tragedies of life, these were said to be caused by deliberate wrong-doing, and the answer then given was to stop doing wrong and start doing what was right. This theory, however, had its difficulties. Many people do very well out of this life although they do a lot of bad things. For a time the Wise managed to stave off this difficulty by saying that even if the prosperous are doing well at the moment the time will come ... (Ps. 73.16-18). But even this did not always work out properly. And it was not only the question of the evil doing well. There was also the problem of people who were good, but who still had a bad time of it. This difficulty was faced by the author of Job, but the first theory remained popular until New Testament times and long after. 'Solomon' makes use of this idea, but he had other things to say on the subject as well, as we shall see further on when his approach to the problem of suffering is considered in more detail. He says: 'Into a malicious soul wisdom shall not enter; nor dwell in the body that is subject to sin' (1.4). Those who are wise will keep the law (6.17-18) they will then know real joy in life (8.16). This is the basic assumption of the author's interpretation of history in chapters 10-19.

The Wise were recognized in other oriental courts before they took their place in the life of Israel. It is one of the most characteristic elements of the Wise that they are international in outlook. Their learning was drawn from many different nations. Because of this the Wisdom writers of Israel are much more sympathetic to other nations than were the prophets. The prophets were very much concerned with their own people, and they realized that God had called Israel in a special way for particular service among the nations. There were Jews who fixed on this and who began to think that all the other nations were evil and would be severely punished at the end of time, whereas Israel was righteous and would be rewarded by God and have compensation for all that she had suffered in the meantime. Over against this were other Jews who fixed on their knowledge of the mercy of God and taught that the Gentiles would have an opportunity to repent and to share the same blessings as Israel. The Book of Jonah is a good example of this teaching. The writers of Wisdom were more in sympathy with this second school of thought. In our own book both views are represented, the international outlook being present in chapters 1-9, and the concern for Israel being greater in chapters 10-19.

One aspect of the international approach of the Wisdom writers was that they began to think about God in rather different terms. In the Old Testament God was very near to the lives of the people. The Hebrew scriptures tell of the way he had helped and guided them through their history. He had his own personal name, by which he was known to them, and like other people he had special characteristics that were his own. He could never be confused with the gods that other nations worshipped. But when Israel's thinkers moved out into the international sphere they no longer used God's name when speaking about him, but spoke of him in a more general way, calling him simply God and sometimes Sovereign Lord or Almighty or some such term. This was partly because God's own name had become so sacred to them that they would never use it. But as far as the writers of the Wisdom books were concerned it was also because this fitted in more with what they had learnt from other countries. They were much

impressed by the fact that God was the God of the whole
world, and what they had to say about him was not simply
true for Israel but for everybody. It was also due to the fact
that the people were no longer as conscious as they had been
in the past of God being close to them. They thought of him
in more and more majestic and spiritual terms until he seemed
to have hardly any active contact with the world at all. No
longer did God walk in Eden or speak through the mouth
of his prophet. Instead he communicated with the world
through angels (cf. Dan. 9.21) or through some other means.

It is these other means that are of particular interest to us
because one of them was Wisdom. This is the point where
the oriental tradition of Wisdom joins on to the Greek one.
The Greeks, as we saw, believed in The Being who was also
very remote from the world. According to the philosophers
this Being communicated with the world through the Logos
(this means the Word). The Logos was the power through
which men were able to reason and to learn about The
Being. It also kept the world going, which is an idea that is
present in Wisd. 1.7; 8.1 but it is 'the Spirit of the Lord' or
'Wisdom' that does this and not the Logos. In fact Wisdom
is more or less what the Greeks meant by Logos. That at
any rate is what 'Solomon' is trying to put over. The idea
that God needed an intermediary of this sort was not unknown in the East. Indeed the Eastern sages went further and
said that God had a feminine companion. In the most ancient
times this was a goddess and it was supposed to be through
intercourse with her that the deity produced the world. These
two ideas, from the West and the East, are combined in the
Wisdom literature of Israel. But neither of them are taken
over as they stand. What 'Solomon' has to say about this
intermediary is thoroughly influenced by the old tradition of
Israel. Sometimes when the prophets did not want to use the
actual name of God they would speak of his spirit. By this
they did not mean another person of the Trinity, as the
Christian does when he speaks of the Holy Spirit. He meant
the power through which God worked on the world. So the

writers of the Wisdom literature sometimes spoke of Wisdom
in terms similar to those that the Greeks used of the Logos
and sometimes in terms similar to those oriental traditions
about a partner of the deity. But all the time what they were
really concerned to say was that this is the way in which the
God of Israel makes contact with the world.

This literary product of our period is usually known as the
Figure of Wisdom, and there is a fairly full account of her in
Prov. 8.22-31. There it is said that Wisdom was 'brought
forth' before the world had been created. She was the companion of God the whole time that he was working and
making the heaven and the earth. Wisdom was a delight to
God and she took a delight in the men whom God had made.
Because of this anyone who finds Wisdom finds the way to
fellowship with God, which is the very substance of life (v. 35),
whilst to hate Wisdom is to court (spiritual) death (v. 36). The
universal tone of this passage will be noted. The writer speaks
of the relationship between God and his creation, between
God and man. There is no suggestion that these words are
intended only for the chosen people. Wisdom loves men. One
of the books of the Apocrypha, Ecclesiasticus, describes Wisdom in the same terms as men usually spoke of God himself.
Instead of saying that she was brought forth before the
creation of the world, Wisdom herself is here thought of as
being eternal (Ecclus. 1.1). She is present everywhere and with
everybody (24.6). But the author also speaks of her as one
of God's creatures (1.4; 24.9). In spite of this universal appeal
the author cannot get away from the idea that Israel was the
favourite people of the earth. Wisdom is summed up in the
law of Moses (24.7-8, 23).

Our author makes use of this figure of Wisdom and likes
to speak of her in the same terms as he would speak of a
woman whom he loves (cf. 8.2). In his greatest passage Wisdom is practically identical with God. Struggling for words to
describe his deepest experiences the author draws on the
vocabulary of the Greek philosophers, though what he meant
by these words was probably rather different from what the

Greeks themselves meant by them (7.22-27). Like God Wisdom is Almighty, All-powerful and All-knowing. In fact, she is so closely connected with the being of God that she is like a breath from his mouth. She is, if you like, the reflection of God, such as you might see in a mirror. Few people could meditate on such sublime truths without being reduced to ?! poetry, and our author is no exception. He is so carried away that he does not stop to work out in detail how one of his descriptions fits in with another. So, whilst Wisdom is his bride she, who is the breath of God, is also the bride of God (8.2-3). The sense of 9.1 ff. is to all intents and purposes that Wisdom created the world, whereas in 9.9 she merely watches God at work.

The author does not invite precise definition of how exactly he pictured Wisdom to himself. But it is clear that what he wants to say is that anyone who knows Wisdom knows God. She shares the secrets of God with him and her will is the same as his will (8.4). This is the real crux of the teaching about Wisdom. It means in the first place that the basis of any real knowledge is religious. To understand the world and to live properly, your mind must be directed towards the maker in worship. 'The fear of the Lord is the beginning of knowledge' (Prov. 1.7). It means in the second place that those who have gone far in finding out God are in the best position to understand the world in which they live. This is where the idea of Wisdom that we have today joins on to the idea of Wisdom as it was put forward by 'Solomon'. We mean by Wisdom a sound knowledge of life. 'Solomon' meant primarily a proper understanding of God. But these two ideas, which we might think of as the practical and the spiritual arise out of and lead into one another.

Wisdom was with God at the creation of the world, either herself the agent of creation or watching God. Who then could be in a better position to inform men about the world in which they are living? 'Solomon' ascribes to her his knowledge of how the world was made, how it works and goes on; knowledge of wild life and the growth of plants are made known by Wisdom (7.15-22). In fact she is the source of what we should call cosmology, physics, chronology, astronomy, zoology, demonology, psychology, botany and medicine. In 8.8 history and rhetoric are added to this list. She is in fact the supreme teacher (7.22; cf. 9.17). If Wisdom was the creator of the world with all its riches in minerals and all the wealth of the fields, who was in a better position to lead men into their possession (7.11; 8.5)? I am sure that this is the right direction to approach the question of material rewards, which troubles some people. 'Solomon' seems to be saying at times that material wealth is not worth much and that he would rather have spiritual qualities. But then he goes on to speak unashamedly of aiming at prosperity. But that is not really his outlook on life. He is saying, on the one hand, that people who make wealth their sole aim in life and who want money for its own sake, no matter at what cost to their worth as human beings, are heading for spiritual bankruptcy; and he is saying, on the other hand, that people who make the fear (worship) of God the fountain head of their knowledge will drink deep of the life that God has given, both spiritually and materially.

Only Wisdom, then, can make known to man the mind of God. She is the source of knowledge and the true teacher. In this case we would assume that the proverbs and the sayings that she inspires would be as clear as crystal. So we are rather surprised when she is presented to us as a great mystery (6.22; 7.13, 21; cf. 17.1). Now why should Wisdom be regarded as a mystery? This might be partly due to the Greek background of this tradition. The old teachers in Greece used to hold classes in secret and they used to take great pains to see that no one who attended their classes told people outside what they had learnt. This was because of the financial aspect: a kind of copyright. If people could find out what they had to say without coming to their schools and paying, then the teachers would be out of a living (cf. 6.22-23). But this then moved in a different direction. Much of what was taught in the schools was what we would call the natural sciences and this led to the discussion of the creation of the world. Here the academic world meets the religious world, where the word 'mystery' was used in a different sense. Some of the rites of the ancient world were called 'mysteries' and they had to do with man's relationship to God, and began with the myths of creation. Now in the Hebrew tradition this did not stop with the creation, but went on to the end of time and spoke of how God would wind up the affairs of men. Later on the people who wrote about this sort of thing were inclined to do so in strange pictures which could well be called mysterious in our present day sense. Books like Daniel and Revelation are of this sort, and take some explaining. Then there was not only the question of the beginning and the end but also of all the things that went on between the two, history. Just what God's purposes were in the world was not always very clear, and those people who were familiar with Wisdom were in a position to explain them. This is what the writer of Ps. 78 means by 'the parable' and the 'dark sayings' that he is going to show to people. So Wisdom is not a clear shining light like the sun that shines on the just and the unjust. It is something of a mystery and you have to be specially trained to understand it. However, 'Solomon' is resolved that it shall not be a closed shop. He is willing to let anyone into the secret who wants to learn. Wisdom, so closely connected with God's inmost being, is in a unique position to make known to men the mysteries of the Godhead.

In 10.1–11.1 Wisdom is spoken of as the power that has guided the world through its history, meting out just rewards to all men. Those who go according to the will of God enjoy the benefits of the world, those who go against his will end in trouble. The story is continued from 11.2 to the end of the book. But here Wisdom has disappeared from the scene which is occupied altogether by God alone. This is one of the factors that has led some scholars to suppose that this latter part of the book was written by a different author. Be that as it may, the Greek concepts of the intermediary between God and the world are discarded and the Old Testament idea of God acting directly in the affairs of the world is resumed.

The Christian reader who has followed this account of Wisdom carefully, may have the feeling that he has heard this sort of thing before somewhere. If so, he is probably being reminded of his efforts to try and understand that extremely difficult but vitally important part of his faith which he has heard called the doctrine of the Holy Trinity. We have seen that Wisdom represents to men the knowledge and the will of God. We have noted in passing that Wisdom is spoken of in some places in the same way as the Holy Spirit is spoken of in other places, and now we shall look at some more instances of this. The connection is made in 1.6-7: 'Wisdom is a loving spirit . . . the Spirit of the Lord filleth the world'. In 7.27 Wisdom is said to inspire the prophets, which, in I Sam. 10.6 for example, is said to be the work of the Spirit of the Lord. Wisdom gives the king power to reign properly (8.14; 9.7 f.), which in the Old Testament is the function of the Spirit of the Lord (I Sam. 16.13). But when the reader reads about Wisdom he will be reminded not only of the Holy Spirit, but also of Jesus Christ the Son of God. God loves Wisdom (8.3) as he loves his Son (Col. 1.13—cf. AV margin). Wisdom led the children of Israel through the desert (10.17) as did Christ (I Cor. 10.4). Both Wisdom and Christ are the 'image' of God (7.26; Col. 1.15). Both are the glory of God flowing out into the world (7.25-26; Heb. 1.1-3). Both are involved in the act of creating the world (7.22; 8.6; Col. 1.16) and of sustaining it once it has been made (7.27; 8.1; Col. 1.17). Further, if the reader will diligently compare our author's description of Wisdom in 7.22-30 with John's description of Christ in the first chapter of his Gospel he will see many connections between the two.

We cannot conclude from this that the doctrine of the Trinity had been made known to the author of our book. Nowhere does he suggest that the Spirit is a separate person of the Godhead; nowhere does he speak of a Son of God in this sense, and it has been noted that he does not always represent Wisdom as altogether separate from God. Nor would it be fair to say that the Christian teachers made up their teaching about the Trinity on the basis of *Wisdom*. What we can say is that when the Church was involved in this immense new experience of God being present in the world in Jesus Christ and of Jesus Christ coming to them again in the Holy Spirit, then in order to express themselves they fell back on the language of this book which was written about a century before. And what we can also say is, that if a person has wrestled with the seventh chapter of *Wisdom* until he begins to understand what it is that the author has to say, then he will be well on the way to understanding that fuller and more glorious revelation that God has made of himself, of which the scriptures of the New Testament and the creeds of the Church are witnesses.

Such, then, is Wisdom traced briefly in these few pages through a development of a thousand years. To sum up we may say that in the beginning to have Wisdom meant to be wise, to understand the world in which you are living. But the sages realized that this involved leading a good life. The life of righteousness was so close to what they understood to be the character of God that they soon thought of Wisdom as stemming from him and in turn leading to him. From various influences which rose both inside Israel and in nations outside, Wisdom came to be described as a companion and helper to God. But so closely was she associated with God in all his work that in *Wisdom* she has the same characteristics and properties as the deity. This became the stepping stone from which the Church could speak of Father, Son and Holy Ghost, three persons, one God.

CREATION

Modern science has led us into a new delight in the world in which we are living. People often feel that Christians do not take this world seriously enough, and grounds for this

In the days of wisdom

impression are not lacking. Those who are trying to find a new life with God are aware that the material things of this life can often do them more harm than good. Preachers are usually much better equipped to talk about how evil the world is than they are to speak of the wonder and the glory of creation. This is due to the deep paradox of man's nature that we shall have to look at more closely in the next paragraph, on man's knowledge of God. The same difficulty was present at the time when *Wisdom* was written. In those days the created universe was attacked from two directions. In the first place there were those Greek philosophers we were talking about. We said that they thought of the material world as a prison in which man's pure soul was locked and they talked of how important it was to escape to a divine and spiritual world. Change and decay was all that they could see here. Changelessness and eternity was what they thought they wanted. In the second place there were men in Israel who had given up this world as hopeless. Ever since the prophets had spoken of the holiness of God the Hebrews had been dissatisfied with the world as they found it. At last some of them were forced to the conclusion that the whole world had become corrupt and evil and that nothing would do but that everything should be wiped out and replaced with a new heaven and a new earth (cf. Isa. 65.17; Rev. 21.1).

The modern reader is, therefore, most grateful to 'Solomon' for taking a strong and positive line in affirming the excellence of the world in which we are living. He appreciated all that there was to be learnt about its plants and the animals and all the mystery of how the world was surrounded by unexplored planets (7.15-22). He was moved by the beauty of the world and impressed by the mightiness of what he saw (13.3-5). He affirms in no uncertain terms that God had made the world (9.1, 9) and he was as sure as the writer of the first chapter of Genesis that what God had made must have been good (1.14). In fact, he goes so far as to say that God loves everything that he has made and that if he hadn't loved it he would not have made it (11.24). No one could speak more profoundly than this author when he says that the purpose of creation is to be found in the love of God for his creatures (cf. 1.6-7).

However, 'Solomon' is not as naïve as people were a generation ago. He was well aware of the fact that all is not as it should be in this world. This was mainly because men failed to work in harmony with the love of God, which was the purpose and motive force of the creation. They became so fascinated by the wonder of what they saw that they forgot to go beyond these things to discover the far greater wonder of him who had made them (13.1). Instead of trying to work in with God's purposes they preferred to use the creation for their own stupid plans, with the result that they made fools of themselves (2.6; cf. 14.11).

EVIL

But this raised its own problems. If God had made a good world how came it that there were people like this in it? This has always been a great problem. 'Solomon' does not seem quite to have made up his mind about it. It raises the whole question of evil and death, and the author was not prepared to admit that these were part of the intention of God when the world was made by him. One answer that he gives is that evil and death were invented by ungodly people (1.16). But this only puts the question back a stage without getting to an answer. In 2.24 he ascribes it all to the 'envy of the devil'. (The exact meaning of this verse will be considered in the commentary.) But whatever he made of it 'Solomon' insists that the world is a good place and that God has no responsibility for any of its imperfections. In another place he traces evil to the time when men started to make idols (14.12, 27) and when the teaching of *Wisdom* about idol worship is reviewed later on, it will be seen that 'Solomon' is again saying what he said in 2.6, namely that where men make more of the creation than they do of the Creator himself, they are well on the way to breaking up the world that they think is so wonderful.

The fact that God made the world was very important for the author. It was not an act that happened a long time ago, and which he could regard with mild academic interest. For

'Solomon' the fact that God made the world meant that God was the one, and the only one, who had power to control it. It meant that God is able to come and direct the course of events in this present time. It also meant that the world was moving in God's direction. The creation is not a collection of atoms thrown together and left to get on the best they can. Man is not a creature deserted on a tiny planet left to sink or swim in the midst of a vast universe. With unflinching faith the author affirms: 'the world fighteth for the righteous' (16.17). This is a faith that the modern Christian must re-capture if he is to be true to his claim that God is King and if he is to share in the victory of Christ. Admittedly there is enough evidence against it. We have seen the nations of the world rise up as great beasts and devour the innocent. Throughout human history man has struggled against disease and famine. There have been times when men have had to cry out that there is no God at all. But the author had seen as much in his own days and the history of Israel had been as terrible as that of any nation. Yet he was unshaken in his conviction that if men could but rise above the darkness of the moment they would see that the world is on their side, and his faith was based on the assurance that God had made the world.

But not only had God invested the world with a moral order. Not only had he directed it to go forward according to his own good will. When necessary he came to re-direct it. He who had created the world in the first place came again to order it afresh, so that those who loved him might be saved. His creation was ordered to help the righteous and at the same time to oppose the evil (16.24). Whilst the sun was shining over all the world God made Egypt to lie in darkness (17.20-21). Creation was re-created so that God's purposes might be achieved (19.6). If only the author had stayed firm in this great affirmation of his faith all would have been well. But he could not resist the temptation to dress up his faith with a scientific theory and he tries to explain this divine activity in terms of the Stoic philosophers who taught that the elements of the world were capable of transforming themselves (19.18-21). That theory has long been discarded as a scientific hypothesis and it should be a warning to Christians who think that the latest scientific theory is going to be a help to their faith. But the belief that God is the Creator and that he is capable of using his creation for his own purposes has no reason to be considered out of date. This, of course, is very relevant to the discussion about the miracles of Christ in the New Testament. The day has long since passed when scientists will say without more ado that these things did not happen because they are contrary to 'scientific laws'. Scientists are prepared to admit that they do not know everything about the world under their observation, and Christians have every reason to re-consider their New Testaments along the lines of what 'Solomon' has to say about creation in this book.

When 'Solomon' came to consider the creation he admired it and was moved to praise his maker. Indeed this was the centre of all that he thought. It was not the creation itself that was so glorious, but the One who had made it (16.26).

MAN

The ideas that men of the ancient world held about the creation naturally influenced what they thought about man, a creature that has always been particularly interested in himself. The Greek philosophers, who thought little of the material world, despised the human body which so obviously belonged to it. The Hebrews, however, never gave way to such thoughts. The Greeks could think of the body as something separate from themselves, their real personality being in their souls. To the Hebrew there was no man without a body. Body, soul and spirit are indissolubly linked together. The Hebrew would not speak of a horrible material lump of clay from which the soul must be delivered.

The writer of Wisdom sees man as Pascal saw him when

he described him as being at the same time the glory and the
scum of the universe. Here was the creature who had been
created in the image of God (2.23; cf. Gen. 1.26). No higher
estimate can be made of his worth than that. Alone in the
material universe man is said to resemble his maker. He is
the prince of the world who is set up by God to rule over the
whole creation (9.2; 10.2) according to the standards by which
God himself maintains order (9.3), sharing in the divine and
moral activity of the deity. But he owes this position of
eminence entirely to the special love that God has for him
(cf. 6.7). Left to himself man is a feeble creature. He was made
from nothing more wonderful than the earth, and at the end
of his days he must return to dust again (7.1; 15.8). Without
God man is feeble, short-lived; his thoughts are miserable, his
devices uncertain; he can hardly understand the world of
which he is a part, let alone the holy things of God (9.5-6;
13-16). Now it is vitally important to the human race that it
should get this very just estimate of itself firmly gripped in
its mind, and these two sides of man's character balanced out.
Irreparable harm has been done to the Christian faith by
eminent theologians past and present who have allowed themselves to be misled by the Greeks and by that aspect of the
Hebrew tradition that belittles the worth of man, especially
as a bodily creature. Whole systems of life have been built
up by over-emphasizing this side of things. Men have defaced
and maltreated the wonderful bodies that God has given them,
marvellously made in his own image, because they thought
that the body in which they were shut up was something evil
in itself. The horror of it is that this monstrous and sacri-
legious teaching is still being put out today in the name of
Christ. At the same time those who have forgotten the low-
liness of man's origin and have emphasized only his glory
have done equal harm in the world. They have become so
obsessed by their own achievements that they have forgotten
how feeble they are compared with the works of God. They
have exalted themselves so high in their own imagination that
they have left no room for God at all. They have led men to

believe that they have no need of a Saviour, for there is nothing in the world that is as wonderful as themselves. The nations of today which have dispensed with the notion of God and have led the masses of the people into material and spiritual bondage are those who have seen man as the first of creatures and have forgotten that he is nothing but dust. The masses of the people who can see nothing wrong with man and think that the whole of religion is a deliberate debasement of proper self-esteem are those who have failed to see that man's primacy is a borrowed glory. By studying *Wisdom* man will be able to get a true focus of his real worth. 'Solomon' does not flinch when he realizes that man's innate being is nothing at all. And yet he affirms all the excellencies that could possibly be ascribed to him. All this because he knows that it is God who has made man what he is, and the real marvel of this lies in what he was before God exalted him.

Having achieved a balanced view of the race the author is able to tackle delicate questions without turning a hair. He comes out unscathed in his comments on procreation. The method God chose to continue life on the earth has always tended to make men feel uneasy. The Greek philosophers thought themselves above that sort of thing and muddled theologians have shared their estimate. Even Augustine was led astray at this point and firmly maintained that the sexual act was abhorrent and evil. 'Solomon' was not so easily shocked by the works of the Almighty. He liked babies and recognized the pleasure of procreation (7.1-4). Some misguided minds have fixed on 3.13 as evidence that the author preferred celibacy. But the verse offers evidence of no such thing. What the author is doing here is to attack an old Hebrew belief that the best thing in life is to have a host of children. He says that virtue is better even than fertility.

The orthodoxy of the writer being thus upheld, it must still be admitted that there are places where traces of heresy are present. In 8.19-20 he speaks of having a good soul that came into a good body. This suggests that there are some bodies that are not good, and this would undo all that we have been saying. It also suggests that the author is speaking of a pre-existent soul. This was a Greek idea, the success of a person in this life being said to depend on his behaviour as a soul before he was born. The Jewish Rabbis were sometimes inclined to speak of some such pre-existence, but of a less personal sort as their souls had not got to the stage of moral choice when they were born. The author is even more daring in 9.15 where he says that ' the corruptible body presseth down the soul '. But in answer to these charges ' Solomon ' must be allowed to plead that he has nowhere said that the body is positively evil and the source of sin. He has only said that it is a hindrance to the spiritual life. In both 8.19-20 and 9.15 he may seem to have made the fatal distinction between the soul and the body which we have seen is contrary to the Hebrew tradition and the truth. But the commentator is sure that the real teaching of the book is contained in 15.11, namely that man is a body into whom God has breathed the power of life (cf. 15.8, 16; 16.14), which is exactly what is taught in the Old Testament (Gen. 2.7). It is not the material world that separates man from God, but the sin which man chooses to do. It would be entirely false exegesis to draw any other meaning than this from 1.4.

IMMORTALITY

There are two popular views today about man's life. On the one hand there are those who think that with death everything is at an end. They expect nothing more, and on the whole they desire nothing more. On the other hand there are those who have a vague idea that everybody is going to survive. Those who hold this view would be hard put to it to explain exactly what is involved in this survival.

Neither view represents the teaching of the New Testament or of *Wisdom.* ' Solomon ' is in no doubt that man is mortal (7.1). But he is equally convinced that death was no part of God's original intention. Just how death had come in he was not certain. In one place he says that death arrived because man's wickedness had introduced it into the world (1.16) and in another place that the devil was responsible (2.24).

But before we can understand what 'Solomon' thinks about the life after death we must consider what the Old Testament has to say about it. We saw in the last section that the Hebrews did not separate the soul and the body. This was true in life and it was also true in death. The ancient world, including Israel, believed in some kind of existence after death. We know this because they used to bury useful objects with their dead, things like pots and ornaments. This belief gave rise to a form of ancestor worship. But there was so much evil connected with this kind of religion that the prophets reacted against it. For centuries Israel was held back from any progress in their understanding of human destiny by the moral implications of what they had observed in others. They came to think of life after death as a kind of shadowy existence taking place in Sheol (which was thought to be below the surface of the earth). There is a very good description of this place and its inhabitants in Ezek. 32. Here the remains of good and bad alike were collected, a reflection of the people that had been, but in no sense souls separated from bodies, and in no sense a continuation of life. But there are passages in the later writings of the Old Testament where an advance has been made on this primitive belief. In a great passage the writer of Job 19.25-27 seems to speak of the day when he will see God after his death. Much clearer evidence is found in Isa. 26.19, though this verse occurs in a passage that was probably added to the book a long time after the prophet lived. In this verse the writer speaks of a time when men will rise from the dead, and by that he means not souls, but the whole man as understood by the Hebrews, that is with the body. There is a further development of this theme in Dan. 12.2. Here the dead rise to judgment, the righteous to everlasting life, the wicked to everlasting contempt.

Going back again to a time a little earlier than Dan. 12.2 we discover the real pivot on which hung Israel's final belief in life after death. The writer of Ps. 73 sings: 'Thou shalt guide me with thy counsel, and afterward receive me to glory. Whom have I in heaven but thee and there is none upon earth that I desire beside thee'. The real issue is not whether man is mortal or immortal. The essence of this matter is the relationship between God and his children. The Hebrew came eventually to the belief that the everlasting God could not be defeated in his purposes for man through the fact of death, which had been introduced into the world contrary to his original purposes.

This was quite a different belief from that which was held by those Greek philosophers who happened to accept a doctrine of immortality. To them man, as he now is, was by his very nature immortal. By this they did not mean the whole of man. His body would die, but his soul would live on. They made no distinction between the good and the bad. They did not speak of a relationship with God in the personal way in which the Hebrews thought of this. Man was immortal because he was akin to The Being, that is to say that his nature was in part the same as the nature of the Eternal.

Now in *Wisdom* the author is writing at a time when these ideas were fairly new in Israel, and there is a conflux between Hebrew ideas, recent and ancient, and some of the Greek ideas. For example, he speaks in places of immortality consisting in being remembered by one's children (4.1; 8.13). This is in effect looking back to the most ancient times when men's lives were perpetuated through the honour that their descendants paid at their shrines (cf. Ps. 112.6; Prov. 10.7). Again, sometimes he looks as if he has absconded to the Greeks and is teaching the immortality of the soul without the body (though only of the righteous, not as a natural property of all men, 3.1 ff.); and at other times he seems to uphold Jewish notions about a resurrection and judgment (3.7 f.). With Holmes one is forced to the conclusion that 'the writer simply added the idea of immortality of the soul immediately after death to one or other of the current forms of Jewish eschatology and did not, or rather could not, make them consistent' (p. 529).

Confused as the author may be over these details, he is
magnificent when he comes to speak about the real character
of immortality. He never loses sight of the fact that what he
is dealing with is a moral issue. It is the souls of the righteous
that are in the hand of God (3.1). Discipline and love and
the keeping of the law are all tied up with the idea of immortality (6.17-19). Immortality is the wages of righteousness
(2.22 f.), or the writer can say absolutely that righteousness is
immortal (1.15; cf. 5.15). But 'Solomon' really strikes deep
when he realizes that this righteousness is not something that
he can pride himself on as if he gained it by his own
efforts. It is the gift of God given to men through Wisdom
(8.13, 17-19). Like the Psalmist 'Solomon' lays all his emphasis on the fact that eternal life means fellowship with God,
and can only be understood in terms of man's relationship
with him. 'They that put their trust in him shall understand
the truth: and such as be faithful in love shall abide with
him: for grace and mercy is to his saints, and he hath care
for his elect' (3.9). To put your trust in God means to live
with him and trusting him as you trust a friend or a parent.
If your love towards God is constant then you will abide with
him, that is with him who abides for evermore. That is man's
response to the grace and mercy with which God cares for his
saints. Immortality means to know God and to enjoy him for
ever (cf. 5.15; 15.3).

This is the essence of immortality as it is presented in
Wisdom, and the New Testament knows no other meaning to
the word than this. Both works reject altogether the belief
that man is by nature immortal. Perhaps this was the original
intention of God. But man by his sin brought corruption into
the world, and with it death. God, however, has made it
possible for man still to choose what kind of creature he will
be, whether he will take his part with the animals and make
a covenant with death (1.16) or whether he will accept his
high calling as a creature made in the image of God, to be
immortal (2.23).

THE KNOWLEDGE OF GOD

One question which worries many earnest people today is how men are to come to know God. They think of friends that they have outside the church who are sincerely trying to find him, but nothing they do seems to bring them any nearer to faith. Others who themselves have a very rich experience of the love of God cannot understand how it is that the majority of people completely fail to see the great truths of their religion. This is a problem that has always stood at the centre of theological discussions. Take any of the great writers from Calvin to Barth and you will find that there is a chapter on the Knowledge of God. It is a question bound up with those ideas we have just reviewed, with Wisdom who interprets the ways of God to man, with the world which God made in its beauty but which has fallen into decay and corruption, with man who is at once the scum and glory of the universe, with his nature which is both of the dust of the earth and of the image of the eternal God; and 'Solomon' has his own contribution to make to this discussion.

In *Wisdom* we find that the ungodly were irritated beyond measure by the calm way in which the faithful claimed to have knowledge of God (2.13). There was some justification for their irritation as there is to this day. Christians are often far too sure about their standing with the Almighty, and speak of him as if he were their personal possession. For what is man that he can know the counsel of God? Man's best is miserable, feeble and uncertain. He can hardly understand the world of which he is a part, let alone the ways of the everlasting God (9.5 f., 13-16). This side of the question is put with force in Job 38.

Now, once more, the clue to the question is moral. It is the fact that man has sinned, that his nature has become corrupt, that makes him unable to know the living God, who is of purer eyes than to behold iniquity. The unbelievers can go a long way in this world, they can have systems of education, high standards of culture and they can get a deal of pleasure out of life. But in the end, 'Solomon' was convinced, they will have to admit that all the way they have gone has been nothing but a road through a profitless wilderness. They will admit with sorrow 'as for the way of the Lord, we have not known it' (5.7). At the present time they cannot understand at all what God is saying to his people (4.17) or what is the meaning of God's acts in history (17.1). The author goes as far as to say that the ungodly refuse to know God (16.16, RV).

There are many today who think that they can come to know God through the world that he has created. When they look at a sunset they have sensations. When they walk through a line of trees that reminds them of a cathedral they have a feeling of awe. These sensations and feelings they interpret as a knowledge of God. But how much of God can we know through them? What do they tell us of his love and his mercy, of his truth and of his goodness? If man's nature is corrupt then his knowledge of God cannot but be imperfect. If nature has fallen from the first state that God intended, how can it now declare the character of the maker? In the passage where 'Solomon' discusses this approach he is pre-pared to admit that a man might know God through his works in creation (13.5), but then he allows himself to be surprised that the human race has not in fact gained this knowledge in that way. The answer to his question in 13.9: 'If they were able to know so much, that they could aim at the world; how did they not sooner find out the Lord thereof?' is to be found in other parts of his book, which we shall look at presently. In fact, on his own testimony elsewhere, the Maker is not revealed to any real extent in the works of creation.

The truth of the matter is that this knowledge is not to come from man's side at all. How could it? Man is mortal. How can he devise the eternal? Man is sinful, how can he imagine the sinless? It is God who leads men to Wisdom and who directs the wise (7.15). The counsel of God is not to be discovered by men unless he sends his Holy Spirit to make known his ways (9.17). The knowledge of God is his free gift to men, when he sends Wisdom to them, and even to know that we come to God through the gift of Wisdom is itself a gift of grace (8.21 RV). No one is saved without the grace of God and grace is the free undeserved gift of God. This is the meaning that Augustine got out of 4.11. The knowledge of God is given to men through Wisdom, who shares God's inmost character, whose will is identical with his will (8.4). The reason why people are unable to come to know God is that their hearts are not right with him. It is not because he hides himself from them. Wisdom does not wait for men to make an immense struggle to discover her. She goes out of her way to meet them (6.12 f.). The knowledge of God starts with God and not with man.

What exactly do we mean by the word, then? When the Greek said that he knew a thing he meant that he had observed it. This is the knowledge of the scientist. He looks at the subject of his study objectively. Any contact with it must be avoided, if possible, and so he studies it in test-tubes or under some protective covering. At all costs he must avoid affecting the object by touching it. Even when he is thinking about it he has to make allowances for his own ways of thinking, because he knows that this will be something that he has brought to the object and not something which is actually in the object that he wants to know. When the Greek transferred these ideas to his religion he felt that the highest point he could reach was to contemplate the deity. When the Hebrew spoke of knowing he meant something quite different. The personal element that the Greek tried to cut out, was all-important to the Hebrew. The word he used for 'to know' he also used for sexual intercourse, the most intimate and personal form of knowing that there is between human beings. God was known not as a cold subject studied in the abstract, but as the one who had loved his people and who had met them in the way and had made himself known to them through mighty acts when he delivered them from Egypt. This is knowing, not in a scientific way, but in a personal way, and this is what 'Solomon' means when he speaks of the know-

ledge of God. This is what people are looking for, though
often they do not realize it. ' Prove to us that God exists '—
this is the perennial cry of unbelievers. What they are asking
for is some kind of test-tube truth, some kind of logical argument which would mean that even if there was not a God they
would have to postulate one. But this would be no knowledge
of the true and living God. To know him means to trust him,
to have fellowship with him, to have seen him at work and
to have shared in his work with him, to rely on him daily for
the gift of his grace. So he cannot be found by those who
distrust him (1.2). Those who stand in a firm personal relationship with God, which is made possible through Wisdom, will
understand the truth (3.9). To know God is to love him as a
father and to be loved by him as a son (2.13, 16). This is how
you know a friend (7.14, 27). The giver is so much more than
the gift, and the creator so much more than the creation, that
these alone will not bring us to the eternal. It is his word that
preserves those who trust in him (16.26).

Now this is leading us at once into a difficulty, and it is
a difficulty that has faced all those who have tried to speak
to men about this great truth of God. Paul was faced by the
same question. How were men to know God? The old answer
had been that you must keep the law of Moses. But he knew
to his cost that this was no answer, because how was he to
keep that majestic law (Rom. 7)? That was just the difficulty.
He knew that the only way to gain this knowledge was for a
man to give himself up to the means God had provided, which
was through the work of Jesus Christ. This a man might do
through faith, through that personal relationship with God,
now made possible through his only Son. This was for Paul
the gift of grace. Now some acute minds immediately saw
the possibilities of this. It meant that a man could go on
being as big a sinner as he liked, so long as he could say that
he was a believer in Christ (cf. Rom. 6.1 f.). The fact that
people can argue in this way shows that they have completely
misunderstood what was meant by knowledge. If knowing
God means being to him as a son then the question of how

D

many sins you may safely try and get away with no longer applies, any more than the question is raised whether you are worthy to be a son. The fact is that because you are a son and because you love the father, you will be trying all the time to live like him, and you will be helped in doing so by the fact that you are living in such close fellowship with him. So the righteous become the friends of God through Wisdom, which in turn prompts in them that way of life which is pleasing to God (7.14). Those excellent virtues that are immortal are the gift of Wisdom (8.10-12, 13). Just as the knowledge of God leads men to act well, so ignorance of God sets them on the course of complete social dissolution (14.22 f.). Envy makes fellowship with God impossible.

This is the crucial point of the knowledge of God and involves with it the understanding of his judgments. Justice is an impersonal affair, and with its nicely calculated dimensions belongs rather to the Greek idea of knowledge than to the Hebrew. If a person is always being held up and criticized, he is likely to get worse instead of better. If a child is always being punished for his mistakes, he will become sullen and will so lack confidence in himself that he will grow up into a weak and unbalanced person. What is needed in education above everything else is not an exact form of justice and punishment, but understanding. The child must be encouraged to overcome his set-backs through sympathy and a real care for his particular difficulties. This is how God comes to us. He does not wait for us to put ourselves right with him before he lets us know him; otherwise there would never be any opportunity for him to come to us. Instead he makes allowances for our weaknesses. He passes over many of our sins, so that coming to know his love we may hate the sins far more than we would ever have done if he had descended on us like a ton of bricks. 'Thou sparest all: for they are thine, O Lord, lover of souls' (11.26). He is not strong to mark iniquity, but leaves time for repentance (11.23). Here, then, are the two great issues that must be held together. Knowledge of God depends on his goodness towards us, not on our righteousness, and yet this very knowledge gives us a better chance of leaving off the old life and putting on the new one, so that the writer can triumphantly affirm: 'If we sin, we are thine, knowing thy power: but we will not sin, knowing that we are accounted thine'.

The Wisdom Literature of Israel has been called the documents of Israel's humanism.[1] This is a more than misleading title. To most of us humanism means a rejection of God from human life. The fact that God's direct action has been replaced by the activity of Wisdom does not take us as far as that. Humanism means the glorification of human things, of the abilities of man's mind, of the excellence of his nature, of his salvation through his own works. In *Wisdom* there is certainly a new interest in man. God saves the heathen because they are men (12.8). Idols are evil because they do harm to the souls of men (14.11). But nothing could be further from the truth than to link *Wisdom* with what is generally understood by humanism. There is no teaching here that human wit and understanding are to be the salvation of men. There is no attempt to build up a moral code through which man by his own efforts may come to perfection. Rather with *Wisdom* we are introduced to those great theological terms which are to be the root of all the best Christian thinking on the subject of man's relationship with God: faith and grace and love and mercy are the foundation of all that the author has to say, and it would be a dull mind indeed that could read his words and not say: 'Surely God is in this place'.

JUDGMENT

The Hebrews were always sure that history had a meaning. God was the Creator of the world, and he was guiding it through its course for some mighty purpose. 'In his hand are both we and our words' (7.16). Just what is happening is not clear to everybody (17.1). On the whole it can be said that

[1] O. S. Rankin, *Wisdom Literature*, p. 3.

God is offering to men life with himself, which is eternal (2.23), but men are able to refuse this offer and go their own way. Those who choose to be with God are helped by him, and those who reject God bring on themselves punishment and destruction.

The punishment may be experienced in this present time. This is the clue to history. Nations that have obeyed God have prospered and those who have gone against God have experienced difficulties. This was the philosophy that was put forward in the book of Deuteronomy. But in the course of Israel's history it was discovered that this did not always work out. Israel, who was supposed to be righteous, seemed to do even worse than the other nations who had nothing to do with the living God and his law. The answer was then removed from the stage of history and put to a time when the affairs of this world would be completed, and men's deeds would be reckoned up. Then the righteous would be vindicated and the evil would be punished. This day was often pictured in lurid detail, for it was going to be a very terrible one (cf. Isa. 24; Ezek. 39). The glory of Israel is pictured in glowing terms (cf. Isa. 60). This day was to be the work of the Messiah and he would have his own kingdom in which Israel would be the ruler. Ideas differed about whether this kingdom would be set up on earth, or whether this earth would be done away with and the kingdom would be in heaven.

The author of *Wisdom* was too balanced a character to be impressed by the more grotesque aspects of this teaching. Indeed he seems deliberately to attack its teaching, especially as regards the practice which grew up and has developed since into one of the pseudo-sciences of the present day, of forecasting the dates on which these things would happen, and in making a great mystery of all the things that God is supposed to have revealed to special persons, whilst hiding them from the rest of his children (cf. 6.22; 7.13, 21). But he does not abandon the fundamental philosophy behind these ideas. He is convinced that God is in charge of the world, and not men, and he knows what the consequences of that will be. At times he allows himself to use some of the current ideas about the glorification of Israel and the judgment of the nations, presumably at the end of time (cf. 3.7 f., 18; 4.18 f.; 5.15 f.).

But for the most part 'Solomon' has his sights trained on the present time rather than some future date. He sees that even now people who reject God are going to bring trouble on themselves. They have not got the seeds of life in them, and even though they seem to do well for a while their labours will come to nothing and their families will not prosper (cf. 3.11, 12, 16, 17). Though they seem to be alive they are spiritually dead (4.16). In chapters 10-19 the author makes a review of history from this point of view. Cain perishes because of his iniquity (10.3); in the flood the righteous are saved and the evil drowned (10.4, 6); Jacob (who is here depicted as being more sinned against than sinning) and Joseph were both the special care of Providence, because they were lovers of Wisdom, and so in spite of their trials they did valiantly (10.10-11, 14). In other places the author combines his sense of the futility of this life for the godless with his belief in a future day of judgment, (2.21-24; cf. 1.16; 4.19-5.14).

As regards punishment in the present time the author has two main things to say. The first is that the punishment is made to fit the crime. The Egyptians worshipped animals and were punished with a plague of them (15.18-16.1). The Egyptians unjustly kept the Israelites in prison. Justly they themselves shall be imprisoned in darkness (17.2). And many other arguments are adduced with which the reader will become only too familiar when he turns to read the text. But the reason given for this aptitude of the judgment is very important. It is so that the sinner may fully understand why the punishment has come upon him: 'that they might know, that wherewithal a man sinneth, by the same also shall he be punished' (11.16). Men must know exactly why they are being afflicted (18.19). The author does not develop his theory any further than this, but we are justified in doing so. Much discussion of punishment, especially in theological circles, omits the important fact that there can be no real punishment without understanding. If punishment is to be effective there must be a moral response in the patient. A child who does not know why he is suffering is being persecuted rather than punished. God who loves all men and is not willing that any should perish makes the punishment so similar to the form of the sin that men cannot fail to see what it is that he is trying to get over to them. This is one of the great contributions that *Wisdom* has to make to the discussion, but the book also links this theory with a less original one, namely that the punishment is made to be worthy of the crime, being exactly proportioned to it (18.4 f; 19.4, 13).

The second thing that the author has to say about judgment is that it is in the hands of God. For the Greeks Justice was a great abstract, an impersonal force that deviated for no man and for no cause. An action having been pronounced just remained so in whatever circumstances. Blind Justice is a familiar figure of the British architectural landscape. 'Solomon' knows nothing of all this. Justice is what God does, and he arranges his methods according to the personal needs and responsibilities of those with whom he is dealing. 'For who shall say, What hast thou done? or who shall withstand thy judgment? or who shall accuse thee for the nations that perish, whom thou hast made? or who shall come to stand against thee, to be avenged for the unrighteous men?' (12.12). But the manner of God's judgment is not arbitrary. It is connected with that principle that was laid down in the last paragraph, that there must be moral response to judgment. Where this is given the punishment may be light, because the people will readily understand. Where there is no response the punishment must be made more and more severe until the sinner is brought to his senses. The author makes much of this, contrasting the different fates of Egypt and Israel. In chapter 12 it is shown that the heathen can understand only the severest reprimands (12.17, 18, 22-27). The Israelites are as children who have been educated with the law, who are familiar with the covenant that binds them to God, and they are but touched with the rod of discipline, and at once they are put right (12.18, 21, 22). Israel was slightly bitten by serpents to remind them of the law (16.5-6, 11) whilst Egypt was altogether destroyed by locusts (16.9). But in all cases God restrained himself, and showed as much mercy as possible, not only to the Jews (12.18, 19, 21) but also to the Gentiles (12.2, 10, 15, 20). God is slow to a fault in punishing, and this is so that people may have plenty of time to repent (12.2, 10).

This is the clue to the history of nations, and the author sees that the same principles are applied to individuals. This was one of the big questions of the time, and what has been called the 'Problem of Suffering' has remained with us to this time. Indeed, the present writer never remembers being present in a study group of students when this question was not raised. The standard Hebrew answer was the same as their philosophy of history. Well-being was the reward of goodness, and adversity must be traced to sin. But the earliest teaching was either that man's faith was being tested or that the subject was being disciplined (cf. Job 32-37). The first of these views at least already implies that suffering was not necessarily the product of guilt[1] though modern psychological research has shown that it often can be. Two other answers were given at a later date. One was that all evil was the work of the devil, and the responsibility was to be traced neither to God nor to man, though this way of escape was blocked at an early stage by the writer of Ecclesiasticus (21.27 f.). The other theory that has arisen, and which has much in every way to be said for it, is that nobody knows (Job 28).

'Solomon' draws on most of the current theories. Suffering is a matter of chastening and trial (3.5-6); as far as the righteous are concerned, affliction is educative (11.10), whereas for the others it is punitive (12.22). But he has also a secret weapon to bring out, namely that the affairs of this life are only a secondary issue. The time of real moment is the future life. An early death in the old days was a sure sign of a bad

[1] O. S. Rankin, *Wisdom Literature*, pp. 19 ff.

life. But now the author can point to an early death as an indication of great holiness (3.3-4; 4.7, 14).

But in the opinion of the present writer the greatest contribution that 'Solomon' has to make to the subject is that he allows all these difficulties to be swallowed up in his overpowering sense of the mercy of God towards all men. Whatever hardships we have to bear here, we may be sure above all that God is a lover of souls, and that it is his good will to spare all things (11.21-26). And I am sure that any real answer to the question must lie along some such lines as these. To the writers of the New Testament there was no problem of suffering. They had seen the most Holy Son of God give himself up in love for the human race, suffering the most terrible agonies that we might be delivered from the consequences of our sin. After this the only glory that Paul desired out of all that the world had to offer was that he might bear about in him the marks of our Lord's passion. Suffering to him was the great privilege of sharing with Christ in the work of redeeming the world to God. 'Solomon' did not have before him such glorious vistas as this. But he saw a long way when he said that the only meaning of history is the infinite love of God towards the human race.

THE VALUE OF *WISDOM* FOR
THE MODERN READER

In the Congregational church in St Andrews there is a study group which is made up of some university students, and some members of the church. One of these members was a teacher before she got married. Another is a baker's apprentice. Another is a shop assistant and yet another is still at school. What happens at these discussions is that the minister sits back and asks the group what it wants to talk about. There is another group sponsored by our church. This is a group of teenagers who for the most part have no connection with religion whatever, and in fact don't approve of it. Their one aim in life is to rock 'n' roll, which they do on the church premises each

Thursday evening without tiring. But they are asked to stay behind afterwards and discuss the world and the church. Two very different groups, but neither of them would wish to be classed as theological, and none of them waste time asking questions because they think they are the right questions to ask. They ask about the things they think really important, things that in their own way they have been thinking a lot about. The subjects which come up most often would probably surprise the average Christian, who spends most of his time saying what a waste of time the curriculum of theological colleges is. They want to have explained to them the doctrine of the Trinity; they are trying to understand the nature of man, whether he is a sinner or whether he is the best possible creature in the best of all possible worlds; they are keenly interested in all questions of life after death; the unbelievers ask how it is that if there is a God we don't see more of him; they are asking how men are to come to a living faith, and what it is that holds so many people back; what is the position of those who belong to other faiths and have not heard about the God of Israel and his Son Jesus Christ our Lord; is the world to run its course for ever, or is there to be a time when time shall cease; what has the faith to say to all that modern scientists have discovered about the present world and its beginnings; how can suffering be reconciled with the belief in an almighty and good God; where and when can we see that God has been active in the affairs of men? All these questions are ones that these people are bringing out time and again, and demanding an answer from those who call God their Father. *Wisdom* as we have seen in the course of this introduction, has something to say to all these things. He has his own answer to give. The Church does not put out this book with any ultimate authority. But the earnest searcher will read his words with interest and respect, whether he agrees with the author or not, and he will have to confess, I think, that 'Solomon' has great things to say, many of them new in his own day, and of abiding value, as spiritually penetrating and as divinely inspiring today as they ever were.

And it will not escape notice that here is a book which many of the writers of the New Testament had on their shelves, and frequently resorted to. I can imagine no Christian who would not wish to possess such a book as that.

COMMENTARY

PART I

WISDOM IN PRACTICE
1-5

GOD IS CONCERNED WITH LIFE'S DAILY AFFAIRS
1.1-16

'Solomon' tells people that God is willing to be found by them. But if they are to have fellowship with him they must lead good lives that would be worthy of his company. Nor should people think that they can escape God's notice. Through Wisdom he is present everywhere in the world, guiding its affairs by the principles of his own goodness, and nothing escapes his notice. So the clue, not only to a right relationship with God, but also to getting on well in the world, is to follow his wishes. Without Wisdom a man will be spiritually dead (11) and this leads in turn to physical death. This leads the author to speak of the presence of death in the world. He is sure that God did not intend it. God made the world a good and healthy place, but men who rejected him introduced death into the world's system (16). In 2.24 the author says that death came in through the envy of the devil.

1. Judges of the earth

As Solomon is supposed to be writing the book he is represented as addressing all the rulers of the earth (JUDGE really means a ruler in the modern sense, not simply a man who sits in court). But the people that the author really has in mind

59

are those aristocratic Jews in Alexandria who had given up
the old faith, and who were using their influential positions to
persecute the faithful believers among their fellow countrymen.

2. tempt

People are said to tempt God in the Old Testament when
they doubt his power (Deut. 6.16), which is what the devil tried
to make Christ do, (Matt. 4.5-7) and when they sin, thinking
that God will not notice (Num. 14.22). Here the word is used
in the second of these two meanings.

distrust

This is the opposite of the faith or trust which is the essence
of a real fellowship with God and a knowledge of him.

4. No division must be made between SOUL and BODY in this
verse. These are just two ways of describing one whole person.

subject

Rather 'pledged'. The metaphor is of a house that has
been mortgaged (cf. Rom. 7.14).

7. filleth the world . . . containeth all things.

This shows signs of influence from the Greek philosophers,
especially Aristotle and the Stoics, whose works were known
by the Alexandrian Jews. These people spoke of a great power
that held together the sum of all things. But the author here
does not mean that God or Wisdom is present in all things,
but that he understands them and knows them (cf. Jer. 23.24),
and also that he maintains them and keeps them going. Christians came to speak about Christ in the same way (cf. Col.
1.17; Heb. 1.3).

knowledge of the voice

The meaning is, of every human voice.

10. jealousy
God is described as a jealous God in the OT (Ex. 20.5). He
is jealous for his honour and for the welfare of his people.
Often the word can be translated 'zealous'. God is keen that
all things should be done for the best.

11. slayeth the soul
This is a reference to spiritual death, that is, being alive in
the body but dead to the things that are worthwhile.

12. The author is saying here what Paul says in Rom. 6.23:
'The wages of sin is death'. For Paul the opposite is eternal
life, the gift of God through Jesus Christ. In Wisd. the opposite is put in v. 15, RIGHTEOUSNESS IS IMMORTAL.

neither hath he . . . living
Cf. Ezek. 33.11.

14. no poison of destruction
The Greeks believed that the world was of its very nature
evil.

kingdom of death
RV Hades. Hades was accepted in Greek and Hebrew
mythology as being a place below the earth where the good
and the bad went alike at death. 'Solomon' would probably
accept it as the destiny of the evil. He certainly had very
different plans for the righteous. The author thinks here of the
dead forces of the world trying to gain the mastery over the
living. In the same way Christ opposed the power of Satan
on the earth (Luke 11. 18-20).

16. made a covenant with it
Death has come into the world because evil men greeted it
as a friend and invited it to come in (this is the sense of the
Greek, which means that they hailed it with their hands and
voices). When the author speaks of covenant he is probably

thinking of Isa. 28.15, but the sense there is rather different. In Isa. men think that they will be protected from the judgments of God because they are allied to the forces of hell. Here death will be the destruction of the people who have introduced him (death is personified here) into creation. Their PART is with death, whereas the righteous have their part with God (cf. Deut. 32.9).

THE ARGUMENTS OF UNBELIEVERS

2.1-20

The author here presents the case of the men who denied the old faith. From his account they were probably young and well-to-do Jews living in the great foreign city who had gone over to the way of life of the Greeks. They had rejected the values of life that were recognized by the pious. They could not see that the life of man was eternal and all their reasoning had to be done in terms of the present life and what is obvious to the senses. As a result they found that life was short and tedious (v. 1). The whole of life is mere chance. We are born more or less by accident when two people meet and get to know one another, and once we are dead it will be all over (2 f.). This puts very well the position of many modern thinkers who have rejected a spiritual interpretation of life. Some of the greatest philosophers of the modern world, who for better or worse have attracted to themselves the name of Existentialists, say exactly the same about human destiny as these young apostate Alexandrian Jews. To them, to speak of divine purpose and a meaning in life is sheer nonsense. Now it does not take a great philosopher to reach this conclusion, and many simple people have much the same ideas. The question is, what to do? For it is clear that once the worth of human life has been reduced, and once it is accepted that this life is a pretty mean thing that will soon pass away, and that it is without purpose, then the great moral strivings and sacrifices of

the righteous to improve themselves are a waste of time. The
answer given differs according to whether you are a philosopher or just a simple person. If you are a philosopher you
can say that there are grave decisions that have to be made,
and you still have to make them whether there is any point in
doing so or not. Simpler people decide that as there is no
point in putting yourself out, and as there can be no such
thing as right and wrong, the thing to do is to enjoy yourself
whilst you can. This was evidently the decision that the Alex-
andrians had reached. COME ON THEREFORE, LET US ENJOY THE
GOOD THINGS THAT ARE PRESENT! (v. 6). They intend to miss
nothing of what life offers (vv. 6-9). On the surface this seems
to be quite a noble point of view. There is no otherworldli-
ness here. People are really prepared to enjoy the things that
God has made, and this is so much healthier than the attitude
which objects to everything on principle. But where it goes
wrong is that they take the world as their own possession, and
do not respond to it thankfully as the evidence of God's love
to man (cf. 1.6). They do not recognize God's work in this
(cf. 1.14). They love the gift instead of the giver, and they
reject the moral purposes of the creation. They are then moved
to an unutterable hatred of those who are living an orderly
life (vv. 10-20). These holier-than-thou people only spoil their
enjoyment of life, and so they will suppress them. Might is
right (v. 11). This is a common psychological reaction towards
people whom secretly we think are doing better than ourselves
in one direction or another. It is also a record of actual historical circumstances. The apostates in Alexandria saw to it
that the pious Jews had as hard a time of it as possible. The
same kind of bitterness existed between the Pharisees and the
Sadducees in Palestine. It will be remembered that the Sadducees also denied belief in the resurrection of the dead. And
Christians have long seen in these verses a description of the
way in which the world treated the righteous Son of God.
They will lie in wait for the righteous because he admonishes
them for not keeping his law, which they find a bore; he
claims to have knowledge of God, and calls himself a child of

the Lord; it annoys them even to look at him. So they decide
to torture him, to put him to a shameful death, so as to prove
the meekness and patience that he is always talking about, and
to see if God will really deliver him from his enemies. This is
so near the Gospel account of the life of our Lord that some
scholars have been tempted to think that the passage may
have been put in later by a Christian reader. But the words are
quite possible from the Alexandrian situation, and they fit into
the course of the author's argument which goes on to speak
of the hopes of the righteous in contrast with this philosophy
of the unbelievers.

1. man . . . the grave
    Christ said that even if one had returned from the dead they
would not have believed (Luke 16.30-31). Or is this an addi-
tion by teachers of the Church after the world had failed to
believe in Christ, even though he was risen with power?

2. breath . . . of our heart
    Read with RV margin: 'Reason is a spark *kindled* by the
beating of our heart.' BREATH here means the principle of life
that moves the body. HEART was to the Hebrew the part of the
body where thinking went on. We would speak of the mind.
Bearing this in mind, compare what Gregg says in his commentary on this verse: 'It is hard to avoid the conclusion that
there is a half-concealed cynical allusion to the speculations
of Greek philosophy. Heraclitus held that fire was the origin
of all things and Zeno developed the idea further. He held
that the soul was a fiery principle with which we are inspired
and by which we move. . . . Its followers are landed in the
cheering thought, that our soul is a spark and our breath
the smoke of its smouldering.'

3. our body . . . soft air.
    The ungodly here state that body and soul perish in death.
The writer of Ecclesiastes seems to have had much the same
idea (cf. Eccles 12.7), and there are some scholars who think

that *Wisdom* here makes a conscious attack on the earlier
Hebrew author.

10 f. The ungodly here determine to do all that a righteous
man like Job did not do (cf. Job 31).

12. the righteous
Whilst this is singular it does not refer to a single man, but
is used collectively of the whole Jewish-Egyptian community.

18. Cf. Matt. 27.43; John 5.18.

20. If this is a reference to a persecution of the Jews in Egypt
it must have taken place about a century before *Wisdom* was
written.

REPLY TO THE UNBELIEVERS

2.21–3.9

' Solomon ' replies that the unbelievers are only able to reason
in this way because they have no knowledge of God, and they
do not realize that man has a higher destiny than can be
obtained from the things of this earthly life. The fact that
there is death in the world at all is due to the activity of the
devil (cf. 1.16, where it is due to the invitation of evil men).
This closes the second chapter and in the third chapter the
author goes on to state the case of the righteous. This is a
sublime passage beginning with the words BUT THE SOULS OF
THE RIGHTEOUS ARE IN THE HANDS OF GOD, but the writer
seems to get rather mixed up with himself. This may be due
to the fact that he starts off with a statement of a belief in the
immortality of the soul, immediately after death, an idea that
was new in Israel. Anyway, he says that the death of the
righteous seems to be a punishment but in fact it is not, because they are in peace and their hope is full of immortality.

E

However, the fact that he has been led to speak of death as a punishment leads him off on to a familiar OT track, that suffering in this present time is no more than chastening or, if you like, it is God refining the character, as gold is refined in the fire (cf. Prov. 3.11-12). However true this may be, it is a quite different theme from the one with which he started. Then, recollecting that he was supposed to be talking about something else, he returns to the final justification of the righteous, but he does so in quite different terms from the ones with which he set out. In vv. 7-8 he withdraws from the new theory of life immediately after death and speaks in traditional Jewish terms of the day when the Messianic Kingdom will be ushered in, and the righteous with their Messiah will rule over the nations of the world for ever. All this muddle, however, is readily forgiven when we come to the incomparable words of ṽi 9. Here the author strikes to the real meaning of eternal life: the fact that man will abide in love with God, and that the assurance of immortality lies in the grace and mercy which God ever shows towards his people. It is impossible for man to picture to himself adequately the precise nature of eternity, and when he comes to speak of it at all he is sure to err. But to state that man's future condition is to be determined by his relationship with the ever-living God is to give voice to an eternal truth.

2.22. the mysteries of God.

This means knowledge of the rewards that have been prepared for the righteous (cf. I Cor. 2.9).

23. image of his own eternity

The difficult words of Gen. 1.26 'let us make man in our own image' are here taken to mean that man was made immortal as God is eternal, thus distinguishing him from the rest of the creatures. This immortality is no longer the property of all men, but only of the righteous as the next verse shows. Also chapter 3 shows that the author realized that even the righteous still experience physical death, but since this is there presented as an immediate transition to the presence of God the significance of death has been overcome for them.

24. This is the earliest known reference to the DEVIL as the tempter. In Gen. 3 Eve is tempted by a serpent which Philo (writing in Alexandria after 'Solomon') interpreted as the passions of human pleasure. One of the earliest references to Satan in the OT is in the book of Job, where he is represented as one of God's counsellors and not as the source of evil. We find Satan in what has become his more familiar garb in I Chron. 21.1 where he provokes David to act wrongly, though in the earlier account (II Sam. 24.1) this action is attributed to God. If this verse is a reference to Gen. 3, then the ENVY must be the devil's envy of the wonderful lot of the human race in Eden, an aspect that Milton dwells on at length in *Paradise Lost*. But more probably the reference is to Gen. 4 where Cain is reported to have murdered Abel because of envy. This is the first instance of death recorded in scripture. Here, the author says, physical and spiritual death were brought into the world. But as regards spiritual death at any rate its influence is not universal. A man may choose whether he will have part with the devil or with God.

3.6. burnt offering
This is a noble place to ascribe to suffering in human life. The author sees it as an offering made by the righteous to God which he gladly accepts (cf. II Tim. 4.6).

7. The meaning of this rather obscure verse is probably that in the great and terrible day of the Lord the righteous will move about unharmed whilst the wicked are being consumed (cf. Dan. 12.3; Obad. 18; Matt. 13.43).

8. Cf. Dan. 7.14, 27.

CONTRASTS: THE UNGODLY AND THE RIGHTEOUS

3.10–5.19

The long discourse 2.1–3.9 in which the views of the ungodly
are set side by side with the hopes of the righteous introduces
this next section of the book which places the fortunes of the
ungodly and of the righteous side by side, sometimes—particularly in the case of the righteous—quite brief comments,
developing into a considerable description of the final day of
judgment.

3.10-13a. The ungodly

To reject Wisdom, that is religion, makes the whole of life
meaningless. This is a truth which many have discovered to
their cost today. The author maintains that evil can only
beget evil.

11. nurture

RV 'discipline' is better. It means the way by which wisdom (here: practical righteousness) is obtained.

12. This is a dangerous generalization, and should not be used
by preachers as an illustration for their sermons. It is opposed
to the teaching of Ezekiel, that the children would not be
punished for the sins of their fathers (16.44).

13b-15. The righteous. These verses bravely attack a firmly
accepted theory of the Hebrews that many children were a
sign of God's blessing whilst barrenness implied God's curse,
and suggested that the parents were guilty of some great sin.
The author maintains that this is not the case, and that it is
better to be virtuous and have no children than to have your
name perpetuated by an ungodly brood. It will be noted that
he is speaking of the condition of a married woman. He is not
advocating celibacy.

13. the sinful bed

The words are reminiscent of Ps. 51.5: 'Behold I was shapen in iniquity; and in sin did my mother conceive me'. But the author is probably thinking of Jewish women in Alexandria who married Gentiles.

the visitation of souls

The day of visitation is an element of the traditional Jewish teaching about the end of time (cf. Micah 7.4). The word usually means trouble, but the day of God's VISITATION would be a time for vindicating the righteous as well as punishing the wicked, and the word is used here in a good sense. At that time the righteous will be rewarded.

14. the eunuch

BLESSED IS THE EUNUCH!—a revolutionary thought, as in the old times the eunuch was considered accursed, and was not even allowed into the congregation of God (Deut. 23.1). *Wisdom* reverses this, by saying that if the eunuch is righteous he will have his inheritance in the temple along with the rest of the people. This thought had already been put forward in one of the later chapters of Isaiah (56.4 f.). Jesus goes even further in hinting that a eunuch may be in a better position to serve God than others (Matt. 19.12, which most modern commentators assume to be meant metaphorically and what is intended is self-restraint, not physical disablement).

16-19. The ungodly. Even though the ungodly may have children their offspring will be no credit to them. The writer assumes that the children will be the same as the parents in their wickedness. They will never come to any good. If they live for a long time the only thing they will be noted for is longevity, and if they die young they shall be without hope, unlike the righteous man who meets an early death (cf. 4.13 f.). Their end will be horrible.

16. adulterers

This is again a reference to marriage with Gentiles. 'Adultery' was a term used in the OT of people who worshipped foreign gods (cf. Hos. 2.2). This was in contrast with the beautiful image of a faithful Israel as a wife of God (cf. Ezek. 16; 23; Wisd. 8.2-3).

4.1-2. The righteous. The discussion continues to centre around children. The author returns to the theme of the righteous who have no children. An ancient hope was that man would be immortal through the memory of his posterity (cf. Ps. 112.6; Prov. 10.7). 'Solomon' says that the real immortality is the memory of virtue which is preserved not only in the mind of men, but also with the eternal God.

2. it weareth a crown and triumpheth
This is a metaphor taken from the Greek games which were a popular form of recreation and originally of religious significance. The author is very daring to speak to his opponents in their own terms (cf. I Tim. 6.12; II Tim. 4.7).

3-6. The ungodly
The author repeats his thesis that the children of the ungodly will come to no good (as in 3.12-13; 15-19) and adds that their only use will be to witness against their parents in the day of judgment. This continual moralizing only helps to weaken the considerable philosophical insight of the statement in 3.11.

3. The reader will be reminded of some of Christ's parables in these verses. With v. 3 cf. the Parable of the Sower (Matt. 13.6, 21).

4. Cf. the parable of the house built on sand (Matt. 7.26 f.).

5. Cf. the parable of the Fig Tree (Luke 13.6 ff.).

6. John 9.2 reminds us that the misfortunes of children were regarded as a judgment against their parents, but this verse

reminds us rather of the part the children will take in the day
of judgment as witnesses against their parents. One of the
reasons why the Israelite wanted many children was so that
they would support him at the city gate where the affairs of
the city were settled (cf. Ps. 127.3-5). 'Solomon' says that the
ungodly are in for a surprise at the last judgment, for all their
children will be there to shame them rather than to support
them. I am reminded of a friend who was being shown round
a mental hospital, and was told by the doctor in charge that
nine out of ten of the patients would not have been there if
their parents had obeyed the elementary laws of Christian
morality. It would be unfair to claim, of course, that this is
the sort of thing that was originally intended in this passage.
The author means that the children of the ungodly will lead
ungodly lives. This is also true.

7-15. The author now draws out another point that he has
mentioned: the question of long life (3.17). The traditional
teaching was that the righteous would live to a ripe old age,
whereas the wicked were cut off early. This teaching he now
reverses, or at least says that it does not signify. He takes
first the case of the righteous and says that if they die young
it is a sign that God is careful for their welfare, and as they
have reached perfection at such an early stage, he removes
them in case they should be corrupted by living in the world.
This is a very beautiful thought. He produces a new set of
values: not senility but virtue and wisdom are the things to
go after. This is something that the ungodly have failed to
understand. They do not know God. They do not know the
grace and mercy through which his people are bound to him.

10. Many have been tempted to see in this verse a reference
to Enoch (Gen. 5.21-24; cf. Heb. 11.5). But this is to lay too
much emphasis on the word TRANSLATED which properly
translated means only 'taken away'. A reference to the single
individual Enoch would weaken the case that the author is
putting forward of the ultimate well-being of all the righteous

(that is, faithful Jews). They were likely to be condemned to
A SHAMEFUL DEATH (2.20). It was after death that they found
themselves at REST (4.7). This verse again reminds us of
Christ, God's beloved Son, who was well pleasing to him
(Matt. 17.5).

13. made perfect

The author may have had the Greeks in his mind's eye
when he wrote these words. Their religious rites were aimed
at making the worshippers PERFECT, that is finished and ready
for their departure to the gods, being full of all the necessary
knowledge to make their way through the cosmos to heaven.
But his main sense is that of being morally perfect, though as
the word is also used of dying, he may also be speaking of
those who have been martyred for the faith in their youth.

15. saw, and understood not

The reader may be reminded of Isa. 6.9 f., words which
were taken up in the Gospels (Matt. 13.14) to the confusion
of New Testament scholars. The force of the text in Isa. is
that though the people hear the things of God they will not
understand them, and this may have been the sense of the
Aramaic on which the Gospel quotation is based. In the
present English translations the NT texts can only mean that
Christ spoke to the people in parables for the single reason
that they might not understand what he was talking about,
which seems unlikely. Here all that 'Solomon' is saying is
that the ungodly have interpreted the early death of the
righteous quite wrongly because they were living away from
the fellowship of God and so were unable to understand his
ways.

16-19. The ungodly

The UNGODLY have laughed at the fate of the righteous in
this present time, but in the end they will weep because of
their own miserable destiny. The writer is now entering into
a passage in which he uses the traditional Jewish descriptions

of the last day. In fact the whole passage can be related to Isa. 14.4-21. Some think that v. 16 is out of place and should be read after v. 14. But this is hardly necessary. V. 15 sums up what the writer has been saying about the fate of the righteous, from the point of view of the ungodly, whilst v. 16 leads into a discussion of the fate of the ungodly who are put to shame by the well-being of the righteous.

4.20–5.14. In chapter 4 the author has spoken about events as seen from this world within the sphere of time. He now takes his theme further to the heavenly court which will take place at the last day. He takes up his theme with the wicked first and then contrasts their fate with that of the righteous. It is typical that in his description of the judgment the author does not allow himself to be carried away with the excessive descriptions of some of the Hebrew writers (cf. Joel 2.30 f.). Though he let himself go a little in 4.18 f., he picks up again here and the scene is presented as a calm and rational discussion presented by the ungodly when once they have seen that the values they treasured in life were of no account, and that now all is lost. The statement looks back to ch. 2. There the ungodly spoke of their aims in life; here they revoke those aims as useless. There they were impressed by the brevity of life and denied belief in immortality; here they speak of the meaninglessness of the way of life that they had chosen. There they spoke of pleasure as the only good; here they see it to have been a great mistake. There they were intent on the persecution of the righteous; here they are overwhelmed by the blessedness of those they persecuted.

2. salvation
here means deliverance from the consequences of death, a fact which earlier the ungodly had denied to be possible and were no longer in a position to acquire.

4-5. accounted . . . numbered
The two words are similar in Greek, and point on the one

hand to the estimate that the world placed on the life of the
righteous and on the other hand to the estimate of God.

children of God
This was their claim in life (2.13, 18), now it is their obvious
right. Christ said that the peacemakers would be called the
sons of God (Matt. 5.9).

saints
A word that we have already come across in 4.15. The word
means basically something or someone set apart for a special
purpose, in this case for the holy service of God.

lot
The LOT of Israel in the OT was originally the promised
land. Later this was developed into the idea of the eternal
inheritance in God which the saints were to enjoy (cf. Ps. 16.5;
Acts 26.18).

6. light of righteousness
Among some ancient documents recently discovered beside
the Dead Sea, belonging roughly to the time when our book
was written, there is a scroll called: 'The War of the Sons
of Light and Darkness', which gives an account of somebody
called 'The Teacher of Righteousness'. The general idea
behind this verse is much the same.

13. The ungodly lacked the seeds of life from the start. Man's
life does not consist of his material wealth but of his spiritual
attainments. These the ungodly never had.

14. The author does not teach of the torments of hell so much
as the extinction of the UNGODLY. This is in keeping with his
main theory of immortality which means fundamentally
fellowship with God. Where this does not take place there is
no life left.

15-16. The righteous

The writer falls back on traditional Jewish descriptions of
a Messianic kingdom to describe the felicitous destiny of THE
RIGHTEOUS. They shall receive a GLORIOUS KINGDOM (cf. Dan.
7.18) and a BEAUTIFUL CROWN (cf. Isa. 62.3; Wisd. 4.2). But
'Solomon' continues to emphasize the right things, namely
that all this depends on the love of God for his people.

17-23. The protection which God is going to give to his people
in the time of trouble at the last day leads the author on to
describe the armour of God, which he does in restrained and
moral terms in vv. 17-20: God will take to him righteousness,
true judgment, holiness and severe wrath as his weapons. Paul
must surely have drawn on this passage for his description of
the Christian's armour (Eph. 6.12-17). The whole creation will
be on God's side. After this the author uses the traditional
forms, talking of the elements which will join in the battle
against the ungodly: thunderbolts, clouds, hailstones, the seas
and the floods and the mighty wind (vv. 20-23). So Israel had
pictured her God as a warrior (Isa. 59.16-19; Ps. 7.13-14; cf.
I Thess. 5.8).

This finishes the first part of the book. The author has tried
to show that Wisdom is the answer to this world's needs. He
knows that this is not obvious to the human mind since to
follow Wisdom involves a discipline of considerable self-
denial, whereas the pleasures of this world offer more immediate satisfaction to the senses. But man's sensual life does not
realize his greatest possibilities and if he will only develop
his spiritual potentialities he will discover not only that this
leads to greater enjoyment of the present world, but also
to eternal fellowship with the everlasting God, and this
'Solomon' rightly considers to be the true summit of human
happiness.

PART II

HYMN TO WISDOM

6-9

In Part I the author has shown what difference he thinks getting Wisdom is going to make to life. He now begins to talk about Wisdom itself—or rather we must say herself, because he describes her as a beautiful lady whom he has decided to woo. He shows that she is the way to all that is good, and to the God who is even more than good. He describes all her charms and talks about the wealth of her dowry. He tells of all her wonderful works. In the last chapter he prays that he might find her. This prayer is stylistically carried out to the end of the book—when the author remembers about it. But since for the most part he forgets that he is writing a prayer after chapter 9 we can confine the supplication to that chapter.

ADVICE GIVEN TO DESIRE FOR WISDOM

6.1-11

In this opening passage of the second part the author sums up what he has been saying in Part I, talking about the practical advantages of Wisdom. God loves those who love Wisdom. Those who reject her will end in trouble. The style of the passage is a rather strange combination of the international Wisdom literature type, and the traditional Hebrew type of writing. As with the Wisdom literature generally the address is made to the rulers of the earth (cf. 1.1, where this address was made in keeping with the fiction that Solomon was writing the book, and so addressing his fellow princes). In the first three verses the author keeps this up well enough. The rulers are men who are great among the nations. Their power has been given to them from above. But the mere mention of the title 'king' was enough to worry the pious Jew of post-exilic times. The kings of Israel had for the most part been written off in I and II Kings as rebels who had taken over the throne that belonged to God alone. As for kings outside Israel, they had only served to torment and oppress God's chosen race. All this comes out in the succeeding verses (vv. 5-6) in which the author states that the rulers have ruled badly, have not kept the law, and have been generally irreligious. As a result there is a sore trial awaiting them from God. 'Solomon' would no doubt have been quite willing to apply these words to anyone who was so misguided as ever to have sat on a throne, but his bitterness is probably due to the fact that he has in mind the particular ruling classes in Alexandria, especially those Jews who had taken leading places in the life of the city, who had shown their active contempt for the religion of the fathers and for those who were still devoted to it. Recollecting himself, however, in v. 9 he returns to the polite address of the opening verses, and speaks to the kings as if they were after all capable of listening to sense.

3. The verse states that political authority was given by divine appointment. This does not fit in well with some later Jewish notions which regarded the powers of this world as being universally corrupt. This is part of the long historical conflict between the claims of the Church and the State. Sometimes the issue is modified, and it is merely a question of which will have authority over the other. So in England the national church is governed by the State, whilst in Scotland the national church is independent of the State. But in times of persecution the division is intensified, and the State sometimes seems to be usurping the authority of God. Christ recognized that Pilate

had his authority 'from above' (John 19.11), and Paul taught
that Christians should be obedient to the State which had been
set up by God as a protection for the righteous (Rom. 13).
When the Book of Revelation came to be written, however,
the Church had received so much evil at the hands of her
rulers that the author adopted the Jewish tradition that the
State was evil and the enemy of God.

4. the law

The author undoubtedly means the law of Moses. But as
he is addressing the world at large he appears to be speaking
of a kind of general sense of right and wrong which prevails
in the world, as was acknowledged by St Paul (Rom. 2.14,
where the phrase that Gentiles are 'a law unto themselves'
means something rather different from what would be meant
by the phrase today).

6. The author does not attempt to establish an impersonal
kind of justice after the manner of the best Greek thinkers.
The lowliest will be shown mercy, but the mighty will be
heavily marked down. There is no set law. Each man will be
judged by his abilities and opportunities. The author's real
meaning comes out in v. 7, where the whole matter is referred
to a personal relationship with God. God loves small and
great alike, but he will not be deflected from his judgments
through fear of human pomp.

WISDOM PRAISED

6.12-20

Wisdom is glorious and never fades away. Above all she is
readily found by those who want her. This is the theme that
is taken up in the greatest of all Christian words, the word
Grace. Man's eternal hope does not depend on his own miserable efforts, but on the God who is so gracious that he comes

to man in his need, on the Saviour who died for men who were
still sinners (cf. I John 4.10). This does not mean that a man
may now go on sinning and all will be well because God is
on his side. He must still be WORTHY of Wisdom (v. 16). But
people will be turned to a better way of life simply by being
in her fellowship (v. 15).

No commentator can resist pointing out that the author
employs in these verses a literary device beloved of the Greeks,
called a Sorites, which means a Chain. This is an argument
so constructed that one thing leads to another until the statement in the first line is finally established in the last line
through a process of what should have been unassailable
logic. If this is so, then the most important parts of the Sorites
in vv. 17-20 have been omitted. Gregg reconstructs the text as
follows:

> ' *Desire for Wisdom* is the beginning of Wisdom.
> The beginning of Wisdom is care for discipline.
> Care for discipline is love of her.
> Love of her is keeping of her laws.
> The keeping of her laws is incorruption.
> Incorruption brings near to God.
> To be near to God is *to be a king.*
> Desire for Wisdom makes men kings.'

15. think . . . upon

The Greek is much more forceful than the English, and
means 'to be engaged with spirit' in some activity.

'SOLOMON' WILL TELL US WHAT WISDOM IS

6.21-25

The tone of this passage is again of the international Wisdom
type, as in vv. 1-3 and 9-11, rather than the Jewish strains
that the author admitted in vv. 4-8. This is no longer an

address to the poor and simple, who in fact are the ones who
keep the law, but to the mighty rulers of the earth. These
rulers are not going to be overthrown; they are to be taught
through Wisdom how to rule for evermore. Wisdom is treated
as a great mystery which has to be made known, rather than
the prevenient grace of vv. 12-16, (on Wisdom as a mystery
cf. Introduction, pp. 32 f.). But 'Solomon' is not jealous of his
knowledge of Wisdom, and he is going to make it known,
for the good of the world.

MAN IS BY NATURE MORTAL

7.1-7

In this passage the king modestly admits that he is mortal.
The writer is trying to show up the people who say that
Wisdom's discipline and her excellent virtues may be all very
well for an outstanding person like Solomon, but they can
never hope to attain to it, and so they argue with themselves
that there is no need for them to try. This is a common
enough argument with those who are aware that their lives
do not come up to the standard that is shown in Christ. There
may also be in these verses a return to the ancient idea, held
in both Egypt and Israel as well as many other countries of
the ancient near east, that the king was not as other men are.
He was supposed to be in a special position being either a son
of the gods and divine like them or, as in Israel, the very
special servant of God with outstanding gifts of the spirit.
'Solomon', however, strongly denies that he had any special
advantage over other men. He even goes into detail to establish
the fact that he was born in exactly the same way as everybody else, so that we all start equal. Also, as men are equal
in birth, so they are equal in death. This leads him to the
conclusion (WHEREFORE: v. 7) that he prayed for Wisdom
which on the surface does not seem to have much to do with
it. What in fact is being said in this passage is this: Wisdom

is not a natural attribute of men, no matter how distinguished
they may be; it is something that everyone has to acquire,
and which everyone is in an equally favourable position to
get. Also, to possess Wisdom, which means to be in a right
relationship with God, is to possess immortality (cf. 6.18-19),
which itself means living in fellowship with God. The prayer
for Wisdom then follows logically from the discourse on man's
natural death. And would that Christians would pray about
such things as these! So often prayers are no more than
demands for material comforts. When people are praying for
themselves at all they would do much better to pray for the
most excellent gifts that God of his wisdom is able to give,
the gifts of an understanding and humble heart, of greater
faith and an immortal hope.

VALUES

7.8-14

The author here states what value he personally sets on Wisdom, as religious faith. He prefers her to sceptres, thrones,
riches, gems, gold, silver, health, beauty and light. Sceptres
and thrones are not likely to have been put in the way of
most readers of this little commentary. But the list includes
things which people value more highly than anything else
today. Wealth and influence on no matter how small a scale
will lead men easily away from their religious duties. Health
may now be at the top of the list. Our age is scared of death
and sickness to an extent that has never been before. Of
course, a right desire for the health of the body is not only
allowed to the Christian—it is one of his duties to preserve it.
But there are times when men are called upon to sacrifice
their health if they are to fulfil some great enterprise, or even
if they are to be faithful in the offices of their local community.
Too often the claims of a vigorous religion are subordinated
to the slightest bodily discomfort. In 'Solomon's' time not

F

only was health regarded as supremely desirable, but the lack
of it was taken as a sign that a man was a sinner (cf. Ecclus.
30.14-16). The author also desired Wisdom above BEAUTY,
that is physical attraction. But 'Solomon' does not turn his
back on the good things of this world. Because Wisdom was
the creator of all things she was able to give him the best of
material things as well. This is true to the tradition in the
OT, where Solomon having asked God for Wisdom was also
given riches (I Kings 3.12 f.). The point is not that one is
wrong and the other is right, but that a man shall have a
sense of values and know which should have first place in his
designs. Further in v. 13 the word RICHES shows that Wisdom
offers rewards that are of quite a different nature from those
that the worldlywise are after. In one of his plays Bernard
Shaw described the difference between heaven and hell as the
difference between a concert of classical music and a concert
of jazz. There is no compulsion about who should go where,
but some have learnt to value one thing and others another,
and what would be a joy to one set would be no more than
pain to another. I will not say which of the two types of
music most corresponds to heaven, for there has been far too
much identification made between Christianity and a particular kind of culture already. But in speaking of rewards both
here and in the NT (cf. Matt. 5.12; 6.1) the moral issue has
been greatly confused by those who suppose that what is
being said is that people should forgo a little pleasure here
so that they may have a larger ration of the same pleasure
hereafter. In fact what is being advocated is an entirely new
sense of values. The fundamental characteristic of these new
values is the desire to know God, and Wisdom's gift is that
she makes men FRIENDS OF GOD (v. 14). To be a friend of
Wisdom is to have a recommendation for fellowship with
God. In this way the great gulf between God and man is overcome. A man cannot make himself perfect as he would need
to do before he could have any sort of contact with the Almighty. But Wisdom is able to draw the two together, and
then a man's life itself improves, through Wisdom's influence,

and makes him more worthy of the love that God has shown him.

13. communicate . . . her riches.

On Wisdom as a hidden mystery cf. Introduction pp. 32 f.

THE SCIENCES

7.15-22a

Wisdom, who is the agent of creation, is in a unique position to teach men about the world in which they are living. This is probably the best way to understand the passage, though the author makes so close a connection between God and Wisdom in this passage that it is difficult to distinguish the agent. He begins by saying that God gave him knowledge of the world (v. 17) and finishes by saying that it was Wisdom who taught him (v. 22). This is possible because God is in any case the source of Wisdom (v. 15). Wisdom, to the author then, is not confined in a narrow sense to religious faith, it involves the whole created order. In this passage the author is speaking of what we would call: cosmology, physics, chronology, astronomy, zoology, demonology, psychology, botany and medicine. These are all founded in the Creator-Wisdom, and she imparts them as sciences to men. 'Solomon' maintains that a man of faith will understand the world better than a materialist.

17. the things that are

This is a term used by the Greek philosophers to cover all created things.

how the world was made

Rather, that which makes the world what it is, or in philo-sophical language: the world system.

the operation of the elements

The elements here means, to all intents and purposes, the stars. But in this period the lesser Greeks thought of the stars as gods who controlled the world and the Hebrews seem to have taken over the idea of them as being at least living bodies, though of course subject to God, and in the NT to Christ (cf. Gal. 4.9).

18. beginning . . . times

This probably means a chronological knowledge established through astronomic observation. Gregg suggests that it means the study of the mystic properties of numbers.

19. The study of the STARS was a long established science among the Babylonians, and their learning was added to that of other nations during this period of international exchange. The reader will remember the Magi who saw a star in the east (Matt. 2).

20. winds

The word can also be translated 'spirits', and the words may well mean that 'Solomon' was versed in demonology.

21. This may well be another attack on the esoteric writers of the time.

22. Wisdom is represented here as both creator and teacher.

THE NATURE OF WISDOM

7.22b–8.1

In this chapter the author has told us what value he sets on Wisdom, and also some of the knowledge that Wisdom is able to impart. Now he turns to the inner nature of Wisdom and tries to describe that. This is an infinitely difficult task as anyone will be aware who has tried to describe exactly what he means by God, or has struggled with the important words of Christian theology such as 'essence' and 'substance'. In this bold attempt 'Solomon' falls back on the terms used by the Greek philosophers, particularly the Stoics, when they were describing the world-soul in which they believed. But the reader must not be so misguided as to suppose that 'Solomon' was describing the same thing as they were. This book never deviates from a firm belief in the God of Israel as he made himself known in the OT. The figure of Wisdom as described in these verses is essentially this God as he is known to men, that is, active in the world. Wisdom is God revealed in his power and glory, in light and goodness. True, the author speaks of Wisdom and not of God, so implying a different person. But this person shares all the essential characteristics which make God God, and this God whom 'Solomon' knew and worshipped was one single God. He would have considered it blasphemy to regard Wisdom as *another* God. She was the manifestation of the one God. She was as much to be identified with him as the BREATH is with the body. This passage helped the Church a great deal when the fathers came to formulate their belief in the Trinity, and as we shall see, the terms used here had by that time been taken up in the NT. When the author wrote down his description of Wisdom, he was given to speak more about the nature of God also than he realized at the time.

22. in her

This could mean 'in herself', that is 'by nature'. But as Wisdom is here described as a person, this probably refers to the UNDERSTANDING SPIRIT which is in her body as in the bodies of all humans.

one only, manifold

ONE ONLY is the famous word that has got into the creed as 'only begotten'. It implies that Wisdom, the creator, was not herself created, but like God is eternal. ONE ONLY, MANIFOLD may seem to be rather a contradiction in terms. The

words are taken from the philosophers who were very much
taken with the idea of 'the one and the many'. They were
impressed by the diversity of the world as they saw it, and
yet convinced that behind it all there was one single under-
lying purpose. Their 'world-soul' was the one that being itself
single was the moving force behind the manifold activities
within creation (cf. v. 27). 'Solomon' describes Wisdom in the
same terms. ONE ONLY also indicates her special relationship
with God: she is not one of many emanations from God of
the sort that were commonly believed in at this time. There
is no other like her.

23. going through . . . spirits

Wisdom, as the power of life, penetrates also rational
creatures. That at any rate is what the Greeks would teach.
But for 'Solomon' Wisdom is a moral and personal being,
not a kind of mechanical part that is inevitably fitted to all
products. There are some souls that she has nothing to do
with: malicious ones, for example (1.4). Here she is said to
join herself with the spirits that are UNDERSTANDING, PURE,
MOST SUBTIL. MOST SUBTIL means scarcely material. The
author sets himself against the Stoic teaching that the human
soul and God are material.

24. more moving . . . motion

Wisdom is the origin of all motion, the power that got
things started at creation.

passeth and goeth through . . . pureness

These are more Stoic terms used to describe the all-pervad-
ing presence of the world-soul. PURENESS is, therefore, a
physical term here meaning once more practically immaterial;
not a moral term.

25. breath of the power . . . Almighty

Wisdom shares in the divine nature. She is like the breath
to the body. The ancients thought of the BREATH as the driving
energy of the body, like steam in a locomotive engine. Wisdom

is as much a part of God as this. She is the effective working power of God.

influence
This should in fact be translated by the opposite: effluence. The image is of a river flowing out of its source. Wisdom flows out of God, and therefore has the same properties.

glory
The majesty of God, especially as it was made known to man. The post-exilic Jews had a word for it, namely *Shekinah*. This was the glory which took its dwelling in the temple, and which had been with Israel in her wanderings throughout the desert, under the form of the pillar of fire by night and the cloud by day.

26. Brightness
In the previous verse Wisdom was described as a river flowing from its source. Here the watery image is turned to one of light (hence RV translates 'effulgence'). The same term describes Christ's relationship with God (Heb. 1.3).

everlasting light
Light is here synonymous with God (cf. Isa. 60.19-20; I John 1.5). EVERLASTING, Wisdom like God is without beginning and without end.

mirror
The author is not speaking of Wisdom as an empty shadow of the divine power, but as its identical counterpart.

image
Another term used of Christ in his relationship with God (Col. 1.15).

27. remaining in herself . . . new
Wisdom, who is the motive power of the world (v. 24) is the cause of all change, though she remains unchanged herself. This again is very close to the prime mover of the philo-

sophers. But the idea had not escaped the notice of the Psalmist (Ps. 102.26 f.).

in all ages . . . prophets
When the early Church came to define belief in the Trinity the Holy Spirit was described as the one who had inspired the prophets in the writing of the OT. The inspiration of all holy souls is here ascribed to Wisdom. Her aim is to make them FRIENDS OF GOD, once more an emphasis on the fact that true religion is to be estimated in terms of personal fellowship with God.

28. dwelleth
This word is used in Greek of the engagement between a man and a woman. The sense of the verse is that of Cyprian when he said that there is no salvation outside the Church. *Wisdom* may seem to put the statement on a much wider footing than Cyprian with his narrowly defined concept of the Catholic Church. But it must be remembered that 'Solomon' was not speaking of Wisdom in any general sense. She is equivalent to the religion of his fathers.

29. The image of the beautiful woman is kept up. She is said to be more beautiful than the light of the sun, for she was before it and created it.

30. Evil is powerless before Wisdom (cf. John 1.5; Wisd. 4.2).

8.1. one end to another
i.e. 'one end of the world to the other' as RV.

sweetly . . . all things
After this profound study of the inner nature of Wisdom the author speaks of her relationship with the world. Wisdom is the immanent power of God in ordering the affairs of the world.

WISDOM'S DOWRY

8.2-21

Having considered the nature of Wisdom 'Solomon' decides
that she is a woman worth marrying. Not only is she wonderful in herself, but she carries with her a most satisfactory
dowry. She is of noble birth, a privy counsellor of God. She
who is the origin of all things is the key to all riches. She is
even intelligent and virtuous, and she is a scientist who can
read the signs of the times, as well as possessing the powers
of rhetoric. She will be a social asset and a good person to
have at hand in the administration of public affairs, and also
a peaceful person about the home. Above everything else
she brings with her the gift of immortality. A good all-
rounder. She is wealthy and intelligent, but a homely personality too, not an officious feminine bureaucrat. So 'Solomon' wants her. But, like all good lovers, he realizes that he
is not worthy of her. Her coming to him is a gift of the grace
of God, and even to know that she is God's to give is a
matter of grace.

This passage is written in the genuine style of the Wisdom
Literature, which was generally addressed to kings as men
specially chosen of God. This is a king speaking of a royal
bride. It stands in contrast with other parts of the book (e.g.
6.4 f.) which reveal a Jewish antipathy to the ruling classes.

2. spouse

The reader will be reminded that the Church is spoken of
as the bride of Christ (cf. Rev. 21.2). The Hebrew felt that his
fellowship with God was of the most intimate kind.

4. mysteries of the knowledge of God

The Greeks were great on mysteries, i.e., esoteric knowledge
which only the initiated might be told. These generally con-
sisted of secret information about how to get to heaven. The

Hebrews, when they spoke of the mysteries of God, meant his divine counsels which he made known to men through his prophets, which generally had a strongly moral bias. The mysteries which Wisdom is said to impart in this verse are the meaning of history and the purpose of creation.

5. On a right attitude to material wealth (cf. above, p. 82).

7. Cf. the fruits of the Spirit (Gal. 5.22-23).

8. Wisdom imparts knowledge of history and is also able to calculate from this what is likely to happen in the future. The author may also be staking his claims over against the Jewish writers of his time who were speaking of the end of the world in very bizarre terms, and as knowledge which they alone possessed.

subtleties of speeches . . . dark sentences
This means that she understands proverbs and can interpret parables.

signs and wonders
These are miracles. But a miracle is a sign from God (cf. 10.16) and Wisdom is able to say what the sign is intended to convey.

10 f. These are the privileges which Job missed so intensely when he was out of favour (Job. 29.21 f.).

13. This echoes one of the most ancient concepts of immortality: that of being had in remembrance by posterity.

14. The idea of a universal kingship exercised from Jerusalem was popular among the Jews who were waiting for the Messiah to bring in his kingdom on this earth (cf. Ps. 72.8-11).

19 f. The modern reader is inclined to be surprised by these two verses. They contain a doctrine that is unfamiliar to us, namely that the soul exists before birth. The idea was, how-

ever, common at the time both amongst the Greeks and the
Jews. But there was a difference between the two traditions.
For the Jews there was merely a stock of souls that God drew
on to people the world. But for the Greeks it was definitely a
bad thing to be born. The soul was then imprisoned in a body
that was by nature evil and undesirable, and his life was then
to be spent in getting out of the body in the best way he
could. ' Solomon' does not in the least decry the excellence of
the body that he possesses; in fact he thinks that it is a very
good one. The verses suggest that he got a good body in
virtue of having had a good soul, which implies that others
have been less fortunate. But this is one of the many ideas
that ' Solomon' took over without working out its implications, and it is used only in this passage of the book. The
point he is trying to make is not actually reached until v. 21,
and it is that, be he never so good as a human being, he is not
worthy of Wisdom, which came to him as the free gift of the
grace of God, which he obtained through prayer. That great
modern theologian, H. H. Farmer, says that prayer is the
supreme activity of the religious soul, because in it man has
fellowship with God as nowhere else in his experience. Wisdom, as we have seen, is the means through which man is
brought into a living relationship with God (cf. v. 18), and it
is significant that ' Solomon' obtained this through prayer.
This helps towards the understanding of a difficult problem.
Why doesn't everybody worship God? The reason is that
many are looking in the wrong direction. Many are striving
through their own efforts to commend themselves to him. But
those who are rightly instructed know that their salvation is
his gift. But then, asks such a one as Augustine, how is it that
all men do not know where to look? That also is the gift of
grace. This is the view taken in these verses, but it is linked
with the act of prayer, and this helps us to see that when we
reduce the argument to a kind of legal battle in which the
justice of it all is set out in cut and dried terms then we are
failing to understand what is involved. God is not an object
that is to be gained through obeying certain rules. He is a

person who loves and who desires to be loved, and when we commune with him, as we can do only through prayer, then the union of our personalities with his, which 'Solomon' and Christian writers do not hesitate to compare with marriage, works that newness of life which we call salvation. To say that a man can be good and so qualify for heaven is non-sense, because heaven means being with God, and a man can only be with God through those means that he has provided.

PRAYER FOR WISDOM

9.1-18

'Solomon's' prayer for Wisdom is now recorded. God and man are set side by side and contrasted. On the one hand is God, of infinite power, the Creator of the world, who governs all things that are, and to whom man owes what authority he has over the other creatures. On the other hand there is man, feeble, short-lived, of poor intelligence, incapable of making plans with any certainty that they will come to any-thing, having a body that perishes, a creature dimly under-standing the world that he sees, and still further from com-prehending the eternal realities. But God loves man more than any of his other creatures. Man is not so wretched that he cannot come to know God when once the revelation has been made to him, if he is willing to receive it. Now Wisdom is the means through which God makes himself known to the human race. She is in a unique position to do this, because she is the consort of the Almighty, seated by his throne. Wis-dom was present when God made the world (cf. 7.22 where Wisdom is actually the agent of creation herself) and so knows the world from the inside and also has an intimate knowledge of God's purposes. So if a man is the confidant of Wisdom he is well on the way to overcoming his own natural limita-tions. Through the means of Wisdom, which the Christian will recognize as equivalent in 'Solomon's' thought to what the Holy Spirit is to Christian thinking (cf. v. 17), the counsels of God are made known to man, and because this knowledge is both personal and moral, the earth is reformed, the divine takes control of the human activity.

1. word
God's word meant in the OT his power at work (cf. Ps. 33.6). The Greek word for 'word'—Logos—was used by the philosophers in much the same way as 'Wisdom' is used by 'Solomon', and in the NT the link is made between the Word and Wisdom, the divine activity that has been present in the world since the creation and is now made manifest in Christ (cf. John 1).

8. This verse refers to the tradition that Solomon built the temple at Jerusalem (cf. I Kings 5.5, 7 f.). There was an ancient belief that there was a plan in heaven of the TEMPLE as it was to be (cf. Ex. 25.40; I Chron. 28.18 f.). There is no need to suppose that the author is necessarily using Greek ideas here, though it is true that Plato spoke of the things of this world as a shadow of the originals which were in heaven (cf. Heb. 8.5). The reference seems to be here for two reasons, first that it supports the tradition that Solomon is the author of this book, and second that Wisdom is implied as the agent of revelation through whom the heavenly pattern was made known to Solomon (cf. v. 6).

15. Is the author influenced by the Greeks again? Many have seen here the philosophers' contempt for the body as part of the material world. But there are two great differences between this verse and the teaching of the Greeks. First 'Solomon' does not suggest, as the Greeks did, that the body is positively evil; he merely says that it is a hindrance to the spiritual life. Second, the author does not suggest that the soul, merely in virtue of being the soul, is divine, as Plato would have maintained. Without Wisdom not even the soul can rise to better things.

PART III

A PHILOSOPHY OF HISTORY

10-19

In Part I it is shown how Wisdom is relevant to the life of individual people as they try to make their way in the world. This is the story of the soul's quest for God. In Part II the author has tried to express the deep mysteries of the nature of Wisdom, her own being and characteristics. There it was seen that Wisdom is not merely an inner light which inspires individuals to better efforts, but that she is the creator of the world and holds in her power all things that are and the ways of them. The author now goes on to show how this has worked out in history. He is speaking now not so much of individuals, though those who have played a significant part in the course of history are quoted. The author is here concerned with the events of nations. He tells of the rise of Israel from being a group of slaves in Egypt into being a people favoured by Almighty God. This he develops as his thesis about the meaning of Wisdom's friendship. In contrast he shows the defeat and the frustration of those peoples who have ignored the living God and who in trying to become the masters of the world have in fact only succeeded in becoming the slaves of the universe. A large section of this Part (chs. 13-15) is concerned with idol worship, which was then the alternative to true religion.

From 11.2 to the end of the book an important change takes place. Wisdom is no longer referred to; God now takes her place as the driving force of history. This has led some scholars to believe that a different author is at work. There is a significant theological factor involved in such a change as this. Wisdom became prominent in Hebrew thought at a time when the transcendent glory of God was being emphasized, and men believed that so great a spirit as this could not have any direct contact with a world so mean and paltry: this at a time when the glory of the creation, such as it is, was never more appreciated. Wisdom came in as the go-between, the liaison officer between heaven and earth. Chapters 11-19 suggest a return to an earlier form of thinking, to a belief in the God who had made himself personally known to Israel through the mighty works which he had done in history for their well-being, by his own immediate action. However whilst the transition in 11.2 is rather sudden, various points must be borne in mind. In the first place, the author has made it clear in earlier chapters that Wisdom is by nature the same as God, and when he speaks of her he is talking of one whose will and whose action is the same as God's. In the second place, in retelling the story of Israel's growth as a nation he was retelling a tale that was often told, which had been handed down in much this form through constant retelling in the religious services of Israel's worship, and that it is therefore possible that the same author might speak of Wisdom as the divine agent, and yet when making use of the ancient tradition might fall naturally into the use of the more familiar ideas. And in the third place, nothing that is said of God here contradicts what has been said of Wisdom in the earlier chapters, so that the conclusion of the book rises naturally from what has gone before, and the reader is not confronted with any serious break and is at liberty to read the book as an integral whole.

WISDOM REWARDS THE JUST AND
PUNISHES THE UNGODLY

10.1–11.1

The author begins his series of illustrations about the value
of Wisdom's friendship. He begins at the beginning, with
Adam, and goes on to discuss all the major developments in
Israel's history up to the crossing of the Red Sea. He is
attempting to show that this is a moral universe, and that
those who use it accordingly are rewarded and those who do
not, bring about their own destruction, which is instigated in
both cases by Wisdom. In the Old Testament, where this
history is told (Gen.-Ex.), the writers were attempting to illustrate the way in which God had chosen particular people to
fulfil his purposes, and as one group after another had failed
him, he was left only with the house of Jacob. This process
is continued through the Old Testament, until of Jacob's
children only the house of Judah is left. And the story continues through the Bible until it is shown that of the house of
Judah only one man was left who perfectly fulfilled the will
of God, Jesus, the Son of David, and that through him the
whole earth is to return once more to the state that it was in
Adam, in which all men are factually the children of God.
But this process is not the one that *Wisdom* is most concerned
with. Our author approaches the question from the point of
view of how people have reacted to the call of God and their
responsibility in working out their destiny, with Wisdom or
in opposition to her. It will be noted that whilst in Part I
the rewards and punishments which were allotted to individuals occurred at the end of time, here they are seen to be
already present within the lives of men.

1 f. Adam is presented in a much better light in this book
than in Gen. He is taken as an example of a righteous man.
The author confines himself to two points: (i) that Wisdom

BROUGHT HIM OUT OF HIS FALL, that is she was the cause of
his repentance. Adam's repentance is not mentioned in the
Bible, but it was an accepted part of the later Jewish tradition.
(ii) It was Wisdom who gave Adam the authority to rule over
the world. In Gen., of course, it was God who gave the
dominion to Adam, but Wisdom fulfils the normal role of
mediator in the present passage. Also the scriptural account
indicates that Adam's authority was given to him before his
fall. Here his position as a prince in the universe is attributed
to his having adopted the way of Wisdom who brought him
to repentance. The author thus provides an example for himself of the benefits that Wisdom supplies to the righteous. This
interpretation of the story of Adam is in keeping with a new
appreciation of man.

3. The reference is to Cain who murdered his brother Abel
(cf. Gen. 4.12-16). 'Solomon' seems to have regarded Cain as
the real originator of evil in the world (cf. notes on 2.24). The
phrasing in this verse is rather obscure, but the author may
be putting the same point that was brought out by Philo later,
that in killing Abel Cain destroyed his own soul.

4. Cain is now blamed for the FLOOD as well. The incident
is used to illustrate the fact that Wisdom is able to preserve
men from the powers of nature, if they are righteous. The
elements are subject to the will of God.

5. The verse is based on Gen. 11; 12; 22, the three stories of
(i) the tower of Babel; (ii) the call of Abram from Babylon;
(iii) his trial in the offering up of his son, Isaac. Abram, of
course, was not alive at the time when the events at Babel
were supposed to have taken place, but he was involved in
the consequences. As a matter of historical interest Abram
probably was connected with the kinds of towers which were
built for religious worship by the Babylonians, and that seem
to lie behind the story in Gen. 11. 'Solomon' was no doubt
thinking also of the Jews who in his own day were scattered

abroad, especially his fellow townsmen in Alexandria, and
he uses the old tradition as an illustration of the fact that
Wisdom is able to keep men faithful even under these conditions. The story of Isaac is used as a supreme example of this.

6-7. Here is the story of Lot (THE RIGHTEOUS MAN) and his
wife (AN UNBELIEVING SOUL). The author's interest in biology
is again revealed (cf. 7.20), but his point is that THE RIGHTEOUS
MAN was delivered from a destruction which laid waste FIVE
CITIES, whilst the UNBELIEVING SOUL was destroyed.

8-9. The author sums up his thesis: lack of Wisdom leads
first to a failure to understand the world and secondly to complete moral collapse; whilst those who accept Wisdom are
delivered from trouble.

10-12. Jacob is now taken as an example of a righteous man,
which at first sight may be surprising (cf. Gen. 27). But two
things should be borne in mind. One is the fact that the grace
of God reaches out to men in spite of their unworthiness, as
'Solomon' has shown in other parts of his book (cf. above
pp. 49 f.). The other is that the writers of the Old Testament
portray their characters fully, without glossing over their
faults. 'Solomon' is able to overlook the shortcomings, because
he is working backwards. He sees the prosperity of Jacob, in
whom the whole nation has been blessed. Wisdom must have
found him to be righteous, therefore, as only the righteous
prosper. Paul would have said that Jacob was 'counted
righteous', because the grace of God found him as he was,
with all his faults, and still worked through him.

10. right paths

That is, the correct road to where he was going. There is no
moral implication in the phrase here (cf. Gen. 28.20).

shewed him the kingdom of God

This is a reference to the ladder which Jacob saw set up

from earth to heaven with the angels of God ascending and descending on it (Gen. 28.12).

knowledge of holy things
In this vision Jacob was instructed in the ways of Wisdom, to know that righteousness ruled in the earth and that God would protect him and bless the earth through his descendants.

11. Wisdom preserved the exiled Jacob from those who tried to exploit him (cf. Gen. 29.15 ff.; 30.27 ff.; 31.7): but another remark that would be apposite to the situation of the faithful Jews in Alexandria.

13-14. Joseph is taken as another example of a man who was an exile from his country and suffered persecution, but was made great through Wisdom because of his righteousness (cf. Gen. 39-44).

13. from sin
Wisdom gave Joseph the power to resist the temptation of Potiphar's wife.

14. the kingdom
Whilst Jacob had been shown the kingdom of God (v. 10) Joseph was given a kingdom on this earth.

perpetual glory
Joseph was one of those whose fame did not perish.

10.15–11.1. The author now turns from the lives of individuals to the story of the whole nation, which being righteous was delivered from those who were oppressing them in a foreign country, through many miracles that Wisdom performed on their behalf, especially the dividing of the waters of the Red Sea. But this too is traced to the activity of Wisdom through one particular person (Moses, v. 16; 11.1).

17. light of stars

or rather ' flame of stars ' (RV), which is a poetic expression for the more familiar ' Pillar of fire ', here identified with Wisdom, just as Paul later identified the water-giving Rock with Christ (I Cor. 10.4).

21. This points back to Ex. 4.11-12, where Moses is shown to have been most unsuitable from the human point of view for the work to which God had appointed him. ' Solomon ' uses this to show that the work of God is done not through man's ability but through the inspiration of Wisdom.

CRIME AND PUNISHMENT

11.2–12.1

The author continues his theme of how Providence deals with men according to their righteousness. For present purposes it must be remembered that Israel is righteous and everyone else is evil. The author mixes up quite a few things in this chapter, and he would probably have done better if he had thought it out a bit more before he had begun to write. His main theory at the moment is that the punishment fits the crime (v. 16). But two things have to be remembered alongside of this statement. First, that in the case of Israel the punishment is always much less than that handed out to the other nations. In fact their adversity is hardly punishment at all, it is admonition and a trial of their faith. Had the author developed this theme further he might have arrived at something more acceptable, namely that punishment is dependent on the moral response that it evokes. The Israelites had been made morally aware through the law of Moses (historically this was given *after* the deliverance from Egypt, but, says the author between the lines, Never mind about that!) and consequently the merest nod was sufficient to bring them to their senses. But the others could only be corrected through the most severe penal-

ties. This is then developed to show that the very same instru-
ments which had been used for the affliction of the others were
used for the benefit of Israel. The second thing that has to be
put alongside the theme that the punishment fits the crime is
the infinite mercy of God, and the author reaches great heights
when he sees, rising out of the confusion and pain of the
incidents that make up history, the final and triumphant grace
of God extended to all that he has made, because all that he
has made he loves.

From this point in the book the workings of Providence are
attributed to the direct action of God, and Wisdom is left out
(cf. above, pp. 94 f.). This belief in God's active participation
in history, whether personally or through Wisdom, is one of
Israel's greatest contributions to religion. The culmination
of this revelation was when God was made flesh in Christ.

<h2 style="text-align:center">REFLECTIONS ON WATER</h2>

<h3 style="text-align:center">11.2-14</h3>

The author goes on in his own way to talk about the punishments that God sends on people. But it will perhaps make
the sense of the passage clearer to put it in the way that it
might have been set out by a writer today. There are two
main themes running through the passage. The first is that
Nature is a neutral quantity. It is an instrument in the hands
of God and he uses it in one way or another to suit his purposes. Thus the same element may be used to inflict punishment on the Egyptians and to bring relief to the Israelites. The
element considered here is WATER. God produced this out of
a ROCK in the desert—the most unlikely place possible—to
prevent Israel from dying of THIRST. But he used the same
element—during the plagues—to bring disaster to Egypt. The
Nile, which was the sure source of Egypt's life and fertility,
was turned into blood. From this, two further points emerge:
(i) that the Egyptians' grief was doubled by the fact that the

element of their punishment was the means of Israel's relief;
and (ii) Israel's thirst in the desert was only a temporary
matter, and had been sent so that they could appreciate how
greatly the Egyptians had to suffer. In vv. 6 and 7 the author
also brings out the theme that the punishment fits the crime, by
linking the plague of the waters turning to BLOOD (Ex. 7.17)
with Pharaoh's command to drown all the Israelites (Ex. 1.22)
—a connection which is not made in Exodus. God's use of the
natural elements is, then, the first major point of the passage,
and the second is the difference of the treatment God gives to
the Egyptians from that which he gives to the Israelites. The
former are seen as hopeless reprobates outside the influence
of God's family, whilst the latter respond to the God whom
they know and love. Consequently, the first are severely
punished, whilst the second are gently chided.

THE PUNISHMENT FITS THE CRIME

11.15-20

The author now illustrates his theme from the plague of frogs
and lice. The Egyptian religion included a host of animals
that were worshipped as manifestations of one or other of the
many gods in which the Egyptians believed. There is no evidence that they actually worshipped frogs and lice, but the
author must be allowed his sense of humour. Anyway, he
wants to make the point that the means of their sin became
the means of their punishment, and he emphasizes that God
in his almighty power might have released the most awful
beasts on them. There were LIONS and BEARS that he could
have used. There were even supernatural horrors, and the
author lets his imagination rove over what they might have
been like: UNKNOWN WILD BEASTS FULL OF RAGE, NEWLY
CREATED, BREATHING OUT EITHER A FIERY VAPOUR OR FILTHY
SCENTS OF SCATTERED SMOKE, OR SHOOTING HORRIBLE
SPARKLES OUT OF THEIR EYES. God could have used any of
these, but he chose to measure his punishments in accordance

with the type of the sin, so that people would know exactly
why disaster had come upon them.

17. made the world of matter without form

The latter part of this phrase should be translated as in RV,
' of formless matter'. This introduces us to the big question
of whether the world was created out of nothing by God, or
whether when he made the world, he was using some material
already in existence and, therefore, to be thought of as eternal.
The latter was quite definitely the Greek view, but other passages suggest that the author preferred the former view (cf.
9.1, 9). The Hebrew teaching is generally represented as being
that God created the world from nothing (cf. II Macc. 7.28),
and theologians have been keen to preserve this teaching because it brings out the fact that God is something other than
the world, that he alone is eternal and the world is his
creature. But it is doubtful whether this was the original intention of Genesis. It remains doubtful, because this was not
a question of particular interest to the people responsible for
the account of creation in Gen. 1. However, it seems to the
present writer most likely that what is implied in that chapter
is that there was something in existence before the work of
creation began. The story is not one of God conjuring up
material out of nothing, but of his bringing to order what had
existed before as sheer chaos. This is the real work of God,
and the OT continues the story by showing how, through his
wonders at the Red Sea and through his law, he continued to
order the whole world according to his purposes and to bring
order into the chaotic and hostile lives of men. If ' Solomon '
understood this he could have written the present verse without being under the influence of the Greek philosophers.

20. thou hast ordered . . . weight

The world goes round because God has brought order out
of chaos and has measured out everything in due proportion
and balance. When he exercises judgment he does so in the
same terms.

GOD'S LOVE AND MERCY TOWARDS
HIS CREATION

11.21–12.1

There can be few passages so sublime as this in the whole of
scripture. For a moment the author breaks away from his tor-
tuous arguments about the workings of providence, and speaks
with unrestrained depth of the love and mercy of God, which,
as at last he recognizes, are poured out on all men, be they
the sons of Abraham or another. The premiss on which he
bases this statement is that God made all men and it cannot
be but that he loves that which he has made. Sometimes God
is so still that people think he does not exist, or at least that
he does not notice what is going on in the world. But the
reason why he overlooks many things is so that men may have
the chance to repent. Ezekiel knew that God's will was not to
achieve exact justice, but that his delight was to see people
turn from wickedness and lead new lives (Ezek. 33.11), and
the apostles have nothing to add to this (Rom. 2.4; II Peter
3.9-15). In this passage the author shows that mercy comes
before justification, and this is absolutely fundamental to any
theological definition of salvation. The idea that the impulse
to goodness must come from ourselves destroys all hope of
our ever accomplishing anything and repeated failure, which
is inevitable, produces a sense of guilt and fear which only
makes more difficult the ability to cultivate a healthy and
balanced life, which is the meaning of salvation. It is the fact
that God is sympathetic to our weaknesses, and deals with us
mildly that encourages us to come out of ourselves and to live
in his light. It will be noted that in these verses the author
has a very positive attitude to the world, as a place that has
been made by God and that is good. This doctrine goes hand
in hand with the belief in God's universal love throughout the
literary period with which we have to do. The writers who
were inclined to look on the world as fundamentally evil were

those who saw all nations other than Israel as a further manifestation of that evil, and saw no future for them other than
the terrors of God's utmost wrath. The clue to 'Solomon's'
whole philosophy is contained in v. 26 THOU SPAREST ALL,
FOR THEY ARE THINE, O LORD, LOVER OF SOULS. Justice and
mercy, life and death, the world and anything not of this
world, depend entirely on a personal relationship with God.
And if men are to love God, it is no less true that God loves
men.

25. called
  That is 'created'.

12.1. On the face of it this seems to be sheer pantheism. Pantheism is an obnoxious heresy that has sometimes crept in to
corrupt Christian doctrine, and is generally held in some
Eastern religions to this day. The general idea is that God is
in everything. In some teachings (e.g. the Hindu) this means
that matter does not really exist at all, it is merely a particular
manifestation of the spiritual. This is strongly opposed to the
Jewish-Christian belief in creation, in the world as something
manifestly other than God, and therewith the freedom of men
to live their own lives as fully developed people in a neutral
world. Nor is there any good reason to believe that 'Solomon'
has slipped into this heresy. God's spirit was the breath of
life which he breathed into all living creatures (Gen. 2.7; Job
27.3; Eccles. 12.7; John 1.3, 4, 9) and this idea 'Solomon'
applies here to inanimate nature as well, meaning, as 11.25
makes clear, that it is God's Spirit that gives being to all
things, not that the actual personality of God is manifested
through them. In the OT God's spirit meant God as he was
seen in action by men. The created universe is the result of
God's action. It is not to be identified with him.

MORE THOUGHTS ABOUT PROVIDENCE

12.2-27

The interpretation of history is continued, showing that
different treatment was accorded to the heathen who could
understand only the severest reprimands (v. 17; cf. v. 18; vv.
22, 23-27) from the treatment accorded to Israel as children,
people who understood (vv. 18, 21, 22). The author is reaching
out to something like Paul's teaching about the Jerusalem
that is above, that is free (Gal. 5) compared with the earthly
Jerusalem which is in bondage to the law. Of course
'Solomon' is still in bondage to the law, but even this is the
freedom enjoyed by children compared with the utter slavery
of the heathen. However, in all cases the clue to history is
the mercy of God, whether in his treatment of Gentiles (vv.
2, 10, 15, 20) or of Israel (vv. 18, 19, 21).

ILLUSTRATION : THE CANAANITES

12.2-11

God decided to destroy the Canaanites because of their revolt-
ing idolatry, so that there might be a worthy colony for God's
servants. This is a (noble) theme that is taken over from
Deuteronomy. It is not historical, since the Canaanites and
the Israelites lived side by side for many centuries. But eventually in Judaism—that is by the time *Wisdom* was written—
the Hebrew religion had broken free from the ancient practices
of the land they were living in, and the author sees this delay
as an illustration of God's infinite patience, and his readiness
to give men the best possible chance to repent. But in fact
the Canaanites were so evil that God's mercy made no impression on them. God knew this all along, but still they had
their chance. This is not the same as a belief in predestination.

There is no suggestion that God had so ordered things from the start that these people would never have a chance to repent. All we are told is that God knew what sort of people they had become and that they were the sort of people who would not respond to his love.

4-6. The author gives a fairly faithful list of the kind of rites that belonged to the old religion of Palestine, including human sacrifice and sacrificial banquets. These played an important part in the cult as scholars have found through the discovery of ritual texts at Ras Shamra Ugarit about thirty years ago.

8. as men
God's mercy was due to the fact that even these sinners were men. This is a new emphasis in Judaism: the importance of man for his own sake, and this has led some to speak of works like *Wisdom* as the documents of Hebrew humanism. But there is a very great difference between a passage like this and what generally passes as European humanism. Here the utter sinfulness of these people is recognized (vv. 10-11) and the redemptive action is not produced through man's efforts to better himself, but from God.

11. from the beginning
That is to say from the beginning of this particular race of Canaanites (cf. Gen. 9.25). The verse does not imply that all human nature is corrupt from the start, e.g. since Adam. The author does not accept the theory of original sin.

RIGHTEOUSNESS AND POWER ARE GOD'S

12.12-18

Men may think that God's action in being merciful with Israel and severe with the Gentiles is arbitrary. But in fact there can be no questioning of God's righteousness (v. 12) for he alone is God (v. 13); in other words righteousness is what God is.

Here 'Solomon' has reached the same conclusion as Karl Barth did after a further two thousand years of cogitation. Barth has shown how false it is to suppose that when people say 'Our Father', they mean that God is something like an earthly father. Rather it is because men know through revelation something of the Fatherhood of God that they have an idea what earthly fatherhood should be like. So with righteousness. We discover what it is first of all by considering the actions in which God has made himself known. But God's righteousness is never other than right, even from the human point of view, because the heathens only get their deserts. So Augustine justified his doctrine of predestination. It may seem very unfair that some are damned whilst others are saved. But this is not unjust, because all deserved to have been damned, and we are rather left wondering at the amazing mercy of God that some should be saved. God's righteousness is upheld by his strength, his ability to enforce what is right (v. 17). Righteousness that is ineffective can be a positive evil. So the League of Nations failed to bring peace to the world, because although the ideas behind it were righteous there was no effective control coming from it. In this way the noble ideas of the founders were thrown into disrepute and the world was in a worse case than before. But God is able to do all things, though for the sake of mercy he sometimes forbears. God is not the tool of his own power. All power corrupts and absolute power corrupts absolutely—said Lord Acton. But God's absolute power is the instrument of his absolute love as he exercises absolute justice.

12. Who shall say . . . judgment
Cf. Job 9.12, 19.

to stand against thee . . . unrighteous men?
This is a daring image taken from the old custom whereby a relative had the right in law to come and demand the blood of anyone who had wronged a member of his family (cf. Num. 35).

17-18. God only answers power with power when mercy would be without effect. God's POWER had often been questioned in the history of Israel by mighty princes who thought that the deity of this little people could safely be ignored (cf. Ex. 5.2; II Kings 18.32 ff; II Macc. 9.4).

THE MERCY OF THE COVENANT

12.19-22

God has used the other nations as an example to Israel. From his treatment of them they have been able to learn about his mercy, which is surely far greater towards his own children than ever it could be to these outsiders. Israel was taught in this way that even under judgment she could look for mercy. It is important to notice the emphasis that the author places on the fact that this treatment was due to the personal relationship between Israel and God, which found concrete expression in the covenant. This kind of relationship necessarily has its effect in a stronger moral character of the people who are received into it. Thus God's mercy shows Israel the way to be merciful to their fellow men (cf. Matt. 18.23 ff.). This is something far in excess of legal exactitude, and far more noble.

MORE PUNISHMENT FOR THE WICKED

12.23-27

Even with the Gentiles God started off lightly, but as they did not respond to such treatment he came at them with A JUDG-MENT WORTHY OF GOD. They had worshipped idols (v. 23 ABOMINATIONS—the standard euphemism) which showed that they had as much intelligence as backward children, and God dealt with them accordingly. But it became clear that he would have to take the matter much more seriously. They

were finally compelled to acknowledge the authority of God
through sheer terror.

27. damnation

As RV: 'Condemnation'. The reference is to the destruction of the Egyptians in the Red Sea.

EXCURSUS ON IDOLATRY

13-15

The next three chapters are taken up with a discussion about
idolatry. The main line taken by the author here is that these
practices debased man, who ought to be more intelligent, and
dishonoured God, who alone ought to be worshipped. This
attack on idolatry follows from the long tradition of attacks
on the worship of foreign gods made by the Hebrew prophets,
especially Hosea. But the ground there was different. In the
earliest days of the Hebrew religion no one denied that the
gods that were worshipped were real gods. The matter at
stake was not one of intelligence, but rather of faithfulness.
Israel's worship of these deities was stark ingratitude to the
God who had delivered her from Egypt and brought her to
the promised land with many mighty works. In this was involved also the ethical issue of the moral instability of a people
who could be so careless of their true allegiances. 'Solomon'
does not for a moment allow that the gods of the nations are
real. In fact he goes to great pains to point out that there is
nothing to them at all. God alone has the right to claim man's
total obedience, and whoever makes himself a slave to any
less than this has dishonoured his own person. The reason
why God is able to carry man's submission is that he alone
is absolutely good, and he uses his undisputed might in ways
of mercy (cf. 11.21-23). The sin of the idolater is to honour
the creature more than the Creator (cf. Rom. 1.21-25). Only
in the last century, the worship of idols was again a prominent

challenge to the Church as she expanded into primitive countries where pieces of wood and stone were thought to be more
potent than the living God. Today we are not faced with this
problem as a living issue—at any rate in the Western world.
But we have not far to look for people who worship the
creature more than the Creator. We are a generation that
having rejected God and adored the creation for its own sake,
have become its slaves instead of its master.

THE FOOLISHNESS OF THE PHILOSOPHER

13.1-9

The author considers first the elements of the world that were
held to be divine by some of the Greek philosophers. He then
draws out the weakness of human reasoning. Why did the
philosophers think that these material things were gods? Was
it because of their immense beauty? Then they ought to have
realized how much more fine was the one who had made them.
Was it because of their colossal power? Then they ought to
have realized how much mightier was the Creator. But the
author can almost forgive these particular idolaters because
they have one great thing in common with him: a love of the
world that God has made. Yet his final conclusion is that they
are to be condemned because surely if they were wise enough
to get as far as they did, there was something wrong that they
did not go on to discover the final truth. There has always
been a tendency among defenders of the faith to point to the
created order as evidence for the existence of God: notably
in the works of Thomas Aquinas. But even Aquinas could
only give us an 'analogy' of God through the creation, not
God himself. Among the ancients Philo tried the same thing
and ended with a being that lacked altogether those qualities
which declare the presence of the God of Israel. Where in the
whole creation can we learn about 'the Lord, the Lord God,
merciful and gracious, long suffering, and abundant in good-

ness and truth' (Ex. 34.6)? The author expresses his surprise
here that the philosophers have not followed on to know the
Lord. But he has shown in other parts of the book the reason
for this (cf. Introduction, pp. 46 ff.), namely that the knowledge of God in a fallen world is the gift of Wisdom and grace.

2. These are the gods of the Greeks, but they had not been
unknown in the history of Israel's worship (cf. Deut. 4.19).

THE FOOLISHNESS OF IDOLATERS

13.10-19

'Solomon' turns now more particularly to those who make
images and worship them. What he has to say is based on one
of the later parts of the book of Isaiah (cf. especially Isa.
40.19 ff.; 41.7; 44.9-20; 46.17). There is much that is evil
about idolatry, but quite apart from all that, it is simply
stupid. Gods are made of material that has been rejected
because it is not fit for anything else. (How strong a contrast
with a true worshipper like David who would not sacrifice
to the Lord that which had cost him nothing, I Chron. 21.24).
Then when this piece of refuse has been stuck up they pray
to it for health, although it is too weak to stand by itself; for
life—although it has less life than they have themselves; for
aid, although it has never had an experience; for safety in
their journeys, although it cannot move its feet, and for the
success of their handiwork, although its own hands are im-
potent.

REFLECTIONS ON A PIECE OF WOOD

14.1-11

The author continues his discourse on idolatry by considering
the uses that a piece of WOOD can be put to. On the one hand,

a man can make an idol out of it through which he hopes to be delivered from the raging of the sea when he is travelling in another piece of wood that he has made into a boat. On the other hand, God really can help people who are in difficulty by giving a safe voyage to their boat, as for example in the case of Noah. This piece of wood was blessed. But the other wood—the idol—and the idolater are cursed of God, both alike being hateful to God. In v. 11 the author makes a very sound contribution to this subject in explaining exactly why idolatry is so hateful, namely because it is detrimental to the well-being of man. This is because the soul of man which ought to have been turned towards God as his highest good, has been directed towards a piece of wood even feebler than the boat he is travelling in.

1. Many ancient seafarers attached an idol to the prow of the ship (cf. Acts 28.11).

6. Cf. Gen. 6.1 ff. In much of the Jewish literature of this time this incident of the GIANTS' intercourse with the daughters of men is treated as the occasion of the fall of mankind. The original tradition may not have been unconnected with the Sumerian lists of kings, whose ancestors were regarded as being of divine origin and before the flood to have lived for thousands of years. Noah is here described as THE HOPE OF THE WORLD.

7. Many of the ancient Christian commentators saw a reference in this verse to the cross of Christ. Such is classical exegesis. The WOOD is the ark, and the RIGHTEOUSNESS means the descendants of Noah.

8. corruptible

Nothing gave greater offence to Greek piety of the best kind than to infer that the Almighty was subject to the change and decay of the things of time. That was why the doctrine of the Incarnation was a major offence to the Greeks.

H

10. that which is . . . punished

This is an unusual thought, that God should see fit to
punish an inanimate object.

THE EVOLUTION OF IDOLATRY

14.12-21

The author now traces what he believes to have been the
development of idol worship, emphasizing its mean and base
origin. He says that idolatry began as a fancy of men, but
developed into mysteries attached to the dead who were represented by these figures. Probably there was some such instance known to the author, as he cites rather a particular
instance, that of a man whose son had died. After this the
custom was established by law, and was a means of honouring
the king who was far away, and so could not be approached
in person, and because of this they eventually came to regard
the king as divine. Whatever the historical value of the
author's first conjectures may be, there is no doubt that he is
right about these last matters. Only a hundred years before
Wisdom was written Antiochus Epiphanes had set up an
image of himself in the temple at Jerusalem and had com-
manded the people to worship him. They responded by
referring to the image as the abomination of desolations. The
emperors undoubtedly saw the political advantage of a cult
in which they were worshipped as divine, a practice which
linked the whole empire together and which kept the emperor
ever before his subjects. During the Roman period the Jews
were excused from offering sacrifices to the imperial idol—a
practice which was, of course, abhorrent to them—owing to
the good services that they rendered to Julius Caesar on the
battle fields. But they sometimes suffered under later emperors and the Christian Church was not covered by this dis-
pensation. Tertullian was one of the Christian fathers who
presented a good defence about this. He says, altogether in

the spirit of *Wisdom*, We do offer prayers to the living God
on behalf of his majesty, which is a much better thing than
burning incense to a useless block of wood. Both the church
and the synagogue have since offered prayers for the temporal
powers under which they serve.

In this passage no direct reference is made to the true God,
but a comparison with the idols is suggested in the terms that
are cunningly worked into the text. *'arche* (BEGINNING; first
principle) and *'aiona* (FOR EVER; eternal) in v. 13; *mysteria*
and *teleta* (CEREMONIES and SACRIFICES; sacred rites) in v. 15;
'emphane eikon (EXPRESS IMAGE) in v. 17 are all terms that
have special theological significance in the Greek world. Also
THE INCOMMUNICABLE NAME (v. 21) indicates the Jewish address
to God in this period. The proper name of God (YAHWEH)
was never uttered, as it was regarded as too holy to pass the
lips of man. Instead various synonyms were used, such as
'The Eternal' or simply 'The Name' or again 'The Place'.

12. fornication

From the earliest times people had spoken of Israel as the
bride of God. This is both a daring and a profound allusion,
showing how deep and real was the fellowship between God
and his people. But the other side of this is that to leave the
service of God and to go and worship idols is equivalent to
fornication (cf. Deut. 31.16; Judg. 2.17; Isa. 1.21; Ezek.
16.15 ff.). Paul takes a similar line with Christians though the
falling away there is to actual prostitutes (I Cor. 6.15 f.). The
author now sees the fall of man as taking place with the
invention of idols.

THE HARM DONE BY IDOLATRY

14.22-31

In a superb passage the author now deals at length with the
evils inherent in idol worship. He has already shown the depth

of his insight in v. 11, where he said that idol worship was
wicked because it was detrimental to the soul of man. He
now goes into detail, and shows that he is not simply dealing
with abstract theology, or his own pet theme. He is talking
about something which directly affects the daily life and welfare of people. He shows, with a considerable amount of historical evidence on his side, that idol worship goes along with
a dissolute way of life, and opens the way to broken marriages
and every kind of social atrocity. In our own time men have
turned away from the service of the living God, and the result
of this neglect of worship is precisely this social dissolution
of which the author speaks, as the cheap Sunday papers show.

23. secret ceremonies . . . rites

The reference is to the Greek mystery religions. A description of the kind of thing that went on is given in II Macc.
6.1-7.

31. the just vengeance of sinners

Read with RV 'that Justice which hath regard to them that
sin'. In other words, these dead idols will never judge them,
but the living God will.

THE EFFECTS OF GRACE

15.1-6

The author has shown in the closing verses of ch. 14 the evils
that follow from idolatry. He now shows the good that follows
from faith in God. Those who know God are by that very
knowledge, by the influence of his presence, turned towards a
better life, which prevents the tendency to sin. A man's self-
confidence is increased and consequently his ability to live
uprightly is strengthened when the fear of retribution and
punishment has been removed. This is the meaning of v. 2:
IF WE SIN, WE ARE THINE, KNOWING THY POWER: BUT WE

SHALL NOT SIN, KNOWING THAT WE ARE COUNTED THINE. This
is both psychologically true and theologically profound. It
contains the whole Christian doctrine of grace, and this is the
meaning of justification by faith. True religion is a real fellowship with God, which is only possible because God accepts us
as we are. Both Paul and Augustine said this, and both of
them were accused of being immoral, and of saying that the
law no longer counted in their teaching and that they were
leaving the way open for men to be as evil as they liked, in
the sure knowledge that this would not make any difference to
God's love for them. But this is not what they meant at all,
because they knew that once a man knew that he had been
accepted by God he would have greater strength and courage
to live a godly life than if he were trying to live by a book of
rules which he knew he had broken and could not *himself*
avoid breaking.

1. 'Solomon' remembers that since 9.1 he is supposed to be
writing a prayer, a fact that it is easy to lose sight of in the
preceding chapters. He ascribes to the Almighty those qualities
by which God has made himself known in history to the
people of Israel: GRACIOUS AND TRUE, LONGSUFFERING and
merciful. Cf. Ex. 34.6-7.

IDOLS LACK THE LIFE-FORCE

15.7-19

The idolater is a materialist. He has ignored what was to the
Hebrew the most significant and wonderful aspect of creation,
namely that man was different from all other creatures because
God had breathed into him the breath of life. As this act of
God does not appear to have been repeated in the animals,
we must expand this to mean rational life. The idolater has
blasphemously refused to recognize this by giving his devotion
to a creature that was less in the order of creation than him-

self, to a piece of wood which has never inhaled the life-giving breath of God, and which can be used not only for worship but for any mean purpose that the craftsman decides on. The result of his religion is seen in his whole attitude to life which becomes materialistic through and through. He comes to treat the whole of life as a market in which everyone is out to make the best bargain that he can.

8. The teaching of this verse is based on Gen. 2.7.

11. Here again Gen. 2.7 is employed, and this is the life that is renewed for the Christian in the new creation of Christ (cf. John 20.22).

12. The author has put the same confession in the mouths of the ungodly in 2.6 f.

14-15. The nations who oppressed Israel are doubly foolish, because they both worship idols themselves and recognize the validity of the gods of other nations as well. This was a relevant observation at a time when the east and the west were coming into ever closer contact and the different faiths were being assimilated. There may also be a reference to the Hellenistic Jews of Alexandria, whose hatred of the pious Jews was even more active at this time than that of the Gentile nations.

15. Cf. Ps. 115.4-7; 135.15-17.

16. Man's own life is borrowed. He cannot possibly hope to instil life into another creature.

REFLECTIONS ON FOOD

16.1-4

The author now returns from his digression on idolatry to continue the parallels between Israel and the other nations

in their relationship to the divine Providence. He links his
opening parallel with his final remarks in the excursus, where
he was talking about the worship of animals. This he takes
up into his earlier theme, that the punishment fits the crime.
In the plagues the Egyptians were punished with the very
animals that they had been worshipping. Israel, by contrast,
suffered only a short time. This was so that they might better
appreciate how much their enemies were suffering. And then
to Israel other animals were given as a delicious food. So we
see that the laws of nature are not inherent in nature, but are
subject to the purposes of God, animals being either a form
of punishment or of reward, according to the decrees of
Providence.

2. Cf. Ex. 16.13; Num. 11.4; Ps. 78.29.

REFLECTIONS ON BITES

16.5-14

The author now takes for his meditation two passages which
speak of attacks by animals, one on the holy people (Num.
21.6) and one on the Egyptians (Ex. 8; 10). He claims that
on the one hand the creatures that attacked Israel were fierce
and might well be expected to have done real damage, but in
fact God did not allow them to do any harm (this is an
idealization of Num. 21.6 which records that 'much people
of Israel died'). The Egyptians, attacked by creatures of much
lesser degree, which might be expected to cause no more
than slight irritation, were killed. 'Solomon' again draws his
two-pointed conclusion from this. On the one hand the Israelites were such that they needed only a slight warning to bring
them to correction. On the other hand the Egyptians were so
base that only the ultimate penalty could teach them anything.
On the one hand Israel learnt to praise God for his grace.
On the other hand the Egyptians were forced to acknowledge

God because of his power. But this is not the only lesson that
the author finds in his material. He is still concerned with his
denunciation of idolatry, and he takes these two stories as
showing that idols could not help the Egyptians, whereas the
Israelites were saved through the intervention of the living
God. It is true that the Israelites had been told to look on
the sacred serpent, but says the author, quite rightly of course,
it was not this object that delivered them but God who is the
Saviour of all.

12. The addict of modern drugs and tranquillizers might do
well to meditate on this verse. The WORD of God is set over
against the various magical remedies in which the people put
their trust. By this WORD is meant the effective will and power
of God. This was the way of speaking of God's original
activity in creation (cf. 9.1) and of his providence in maintain-
ing what he has created (cf. 16.26; Ps. 107.20; 147.15). The
author maintains, therefore, that a sick man's best policy is
to turn to him who is the Creator, and so the source of life and
health. This is a point which is being taken up more and more
by students of modern medicine.

13-14. The author speaks here after the manner of men, for-
getting his belief in immortality. He falls back on very early
Hebrew ideas about the destiny of man. When a man was
sick the ancients thought that this was the mark that he was
being claimed by the kingdom of death. As one great scholar
has put it: 'As it is possible to be more or less alive, so one
is able to be more or less dead' (J. Pederesen, *Israel I-II*,
1926, E.T., p. 180). The GATES OF HELL, therefore, refer to
sickness (cf. Ps. 86.13), and the verse (13) expands the thought
in v. 12. God is able to deliver men from sickness and bring
them back to health. V. 14 points out that men themselves, on
the other hand, are only able to destroy life.

REFLECTIONS ON RAIN

16.15-29

The clarity of thought, form and expression which are characteristic of earlier parts of the book seem to go awry in this
passage. Really what the author is comparing is things that
come down from heaven, on the one hand the thunderbolts
and lightning with the accompanying storm-rain, and on the
other hand the manna, the delicious food of angels. The first
came to destroy the Egyptians, and the second to save and to
nourish the Israelites. Again it is argued that the natural properties of the elements are not set in them unalterably, but
they are subject to the will of the Creator. On the one hand
FIRE (lightning) burnt all the more strongly in WATER (rain,
its natural enemy) so that the Egyptians might be more truly
punished (vv. 16-18); on the other hand the fire forgot its
power for the benefit of the righteous since the SNOW AND
ICE (i.e. manna, cf. Ex. 16.14) did not melt in the fire (i.e. the
hearths where it was cooked), though it immediately melted
in the morning sun (cf. Ex. 16.21) (vv. 22-23; 27). The section
closes with two homilies based on this *midrash*: that thanksgiving should be offered by the righteous at dawn and that
the ungodly will perish as quickly as the FROST.

20 f. An old tradition had it that the manna tasted of whatever
food the eater preferred.

REFLECTIONS ON NIGHT AND DAY

17.1–18.4

The contrast is now made between the Egyptians who suffered
from a plague of darkness at unnatural times, and the Israelites who were blessed with light at all times. This was a fate

which, in the opinion of 'Solomon', the Egyptians well deserved (18.4). The ideas that lie behind this section are very ancient. The NIGHT was regarded as a manifestation of the primaeval powers of chaos and to be part of the kingdom of death (cf. v. 14). As such the Israelites were immune from its powers because they were under the protection of the Lord. Such conceptions may well be present in the original tradition in Ex. 14.20, where textual emendation based on Kittel's footnotes to the Hebrew text could render the end of the verse as: 'There was cloud and darkness, but it was light all the night for the Israelites'. The confusion noted in the previous section, however, continues here, for in 17.20 f. it is suggested that the Egyptians were afflicted with darkness whilst the rest of the world was enjoying light, whereas in 18.1, 3 the suggestion is that Israel alone enjoyed the benefits of the LIGHT, whilst the rest of the world was in DARKNESS. Finally the theme is spiritualized and the light made to refer to the LAW. This places the Law, and the mission of Israel, on a very high level. The verse no longer pictures Israel as a peculiar people, shut up and jealously guarding her sacred rights and privileges, but rather as one to whom has been entrusted the glorious task of making known to the world the revelation of the living God that she has received (18.4). This gives the author the opportunity to draw out from the preceding story one of his main themes, namely that the punishment fits the crime. Egypt was worthily kept in darkness, because she had shut up in the darkness of prison those who bore the light of the world.

In the midst of all this the author digresses on quite a notable discussion of fear (17.9-19). This he regards as the product of wickedness and cowardice, that make things seem much worse than they are. This leads to the second theme being underlined, namely that the elements serve the purposes of God, since things that are quite natural and under normal conditions would cause no alarm, now put the fear of death into the Egyptians (v. 19).

1. As has been made clear in earlier parts of the book, it is the part of Wisdom to justify the ways of God to man. Without this divine grace a man cannot expect to understand the ways of God for himself.

2. exiled from eternal providence
The darkness acted as a screen between God and the Egyptians.

3. secret sins
The English reader will doubtless at once think of the 'secret faults' of the Psalmist (Ps. 19.12), but since the original intention of the Ps. is probably other than the English reader would suppose, and since in any case the Psalmist would mean something quite other than 'Solomon', the reader, whoever he is, will do well to divest himself of this thought as quickly as possible. The SECRET SINS intended here are without doubt the mystery rites that have been mentioned by the author in 14.23.

7. reproved with disgrace
This is the final report on the Egyptian magicians, who were thought to be every bit as good as Moses when it came to doing wonders, but were now seen to be helpless to deliver the people from the plague of darkness (cf. Isa. 19.3, 11).

21. darkness
That is, hell (cf. v. 14, and the introductory remarks above).

18.1. because they also . . . happy
Read as RV, 'counted it a happy thing that they too had suffered.' The meaning is that the Egyptians heard the noise that the Israelites were making, and because they were unable to see them through the darkness assumed that they were suffering in the same way as themselves, and were glad of it.

2. The Egyptians thank the Israelites for not taking this God-given opportunity of getting their own back by doing evil to them.

4. Cf. Isa. 2.3.

SUITABLE PUNISHMENT FOR THE EGYPTIANS

18.5-19

The Egyptians decided to destroy the children of the Hebrews. Their plans only got so far as one child being taken away (Moses) and he was delivered. Nevertheless, God followed up their intention with a suitable punishment and destroyed all the firstborn of the Egyptians. A further point of contrast is drawn out. The Israelites were warned in dreams about what was going to happen, so that they need have no fear on that night (v. 6). The Egyptians were warned in dreams so that they might understand why they were being punished. This latter is an important point in the author's argument which we have noted before, and is to the effect that there can be no punishment without moral understanding. Vv. 6 and 9 should be read in RV: 'That, having sure knowledge, they might be cheered by the oaths which they had trusted . . . With one consent they took upon themselves the covenant of the divine law'. These phrases are important, underlining as they do the basis of the author's argument. His claim that the treatment of the Egyptians was fair enough is superficial in comparison with his real insight that the treatment of Israel was the result of the particular and personal relationship which they enjoyed with the deity. However, it must be admitted that this passage falls a long way short of the revelation of God as it is found in the scriptures of the Old Testament. In v. 8 it is said that the punishment of Egypt effected the glory of Israel. Ezekiel, on the contrary, had been at pains to point out that the events of the Exodus were to the glory of God, and not for the sake of Israel who had been altogether unworthy of his mighty acts of deliverance (16. 59-63; 20.9, 14, 22, 44). Again, 'Solomon' allows the Egyptians to admit, rather grudgingly and in a state of terror, that the Israelites are THE SONS OF GOD (v. 13), which falls a long way short of Isaiah's oracle of the Egyptians finally joining, willingly and gladly, in the worship of the true God (19.19-25).

9. The description of the events in this verse indicates the celebration of the Passover as it would be observed by the Jews in the time of 'Solomon', and by our Lord a little later (cf. Mark 14) and by Jews to this day, but not as it could have been during the actual historical events (cf. Ex. 12.27, 46; Num, 9.2; Deut. 16.5). The Law was not given until later, but it has always been an important part of the established celebrations. Also the Psalms (SONGS OF PRAISE) were incorporated in the festival in due course of time (cf. Mark 14.26).

9-10. The author continues to make his contrasts, this time between harmony and discord (cf. RV: 'But there sounded back in discord the cry of the enemies').

13. Cf. Ex. 4.22.

14-15. We have already come across the WORD as the action of God in creation (9.1) and in the preservation of what he has made (16.12, 26). In the present verse the WORD is personified, as had already happened in the OT (e.g. Isa. 55.10 f.; Ps. 33.6; 147.15). In the second century, the Christian theologian, Ignatius of Antioch, gave these verses a Christological content. He maintained that, before creation, God existed in silence, and that when he sent out his Word (=Christ) the world was brought into being.

16. A description of the Angel of Death (cf. I Chron. 21.16).

THE HIGH-PRIEST

18.20-25

'Solomon' is rather weak, as we have seen, when dealing with
the revelation as regards the heathen. But he is always superb
when he comes to speak of God's revelation through the
covenant with his people. He now sets Israel in contrast with
the Egyptians once more. The subject is death. He has described how the firstborn of the heathen were wiped out by
death, and this puts him in mind of the fact that the Israelites
had a certain amount of trouble in this direction as well (cf.
Num. 16.44-50). But as usual when speaking of his own
people, he minimizes both the cause and the effects of this
incident. This, in any case, is not his main point. What he is
interested in here is the way in which death was opposed, by
the Egyptians unsuccessfully, through various magic arts, by
the Israelites through the Almighty Word (v. 22; cf. above on
v. 15) in connection with the OATHS and COVENANTS. The word
was invoked by Aaron, whom 'Solomon' would identify with
the high-priest of his own day, though the office as such was
a creation of the fifth or sixth century BC. The plague was
dispensed with through the medium of incense and prayer,
though this is not to be regarded as an Israelite version of
Egyptian magic, since the real power at work is the WORD,
the action of God. But 'Solomon' has moved far from the
primitive conception of Aaron, and indeed of the place of
Israel as a whole in history. This office is no longer relative
to the needs of Israel alone, but comprehends the whole universe, (v. 22). Aaron wore a breastplate with four rows of
three jewels, representing the twelve tribes of Israel (Ex.
28.15 ff.). But since 'Solomon' saw the LONG GARMENT as
representing the WORLD, he may well have thought of the
FOUR ROWS as representing the four elements which in Greek
philosophy were regarded as composing the cosmos. This was

an office which the king of Tyre presumptuously claimed as his own (Ezek. 28).

THE EXODUS RECALLED

19.1-17

The author draws to a close by considering the whole drama of the Exodus, and making a final statement of his two main themes: that the Egyptians got what they deserved and were treated with the severity that was the only thing that would penetrate their dull minds; and that the world was used by God either to overwhelm the Egyptians or to save the Israelites. V. 1 does not necessarily uphold a doctrine of predestination. God knew what the Egyptains would do, but there is no suggestion that he made them do it. In fact v. 4 (where RV 'doom' should be read for DESTINY) indicates that the wrath was something the Egyptians drew on themselves by constantly making things worse instead of better.

6. The Greek philosophers were the first to propound that matter can neither be created nor destroyed, but only changed. 'Solomon' makes use of this notion. But he has far more to say on the subject than the Greeks. He sees the creation as being still at the service of the Creator, and its motion is according to his will.

17. the righteous man.
   Lot, cf. Gen. 19.11.

SCIENCE AND RELIGION

19.18-22

Finally the author expands his scientific data about the changing of the elements. It would make all this exciting history of miracles comprehensible to the enlightened minds of the time. But ' Solomon ' remains a theologian to the end, and he leaves us with the great thought that God is working in history on behalf of his people. We have seen that Ezekiel reached greater heights when he saw that the meaning of history was the glory of God and not of Israel. We might wish that ' Solomon ' had had something to say at the last about the wider visions of his faith that reached out to all men. But we can remain grateful for what it is that he does have to say, and remembering that the burning point of the revelation that God has made of himself to men has been the relationship that he has established with them as men, accepting their limitations as real persons tied down to the particular events of history, we may offer up his prayer with thanksgiving:

FOR IN ALL THINGS, O LORD, THOU DIDST MAGNIFY
THY PEOPLE, AND GLORIFY THEM, NEITHER DIDST THOU
LIGHTLY REGARD THEM: BUT DIDST
ASSIST THEM IN EVERY
TIME AND PLACE.